WEEKEND
WOODWORKING

WEEKEND
WOODWORKING
PLANS & PROJECTS

THE GUILD OF MASTER CRAFTSMAN PUBLICATIONS

First published 2016 by
Guild of Master Craftsman Publications Ltd
Castle Place, 166 High Street, Lewes,
East Sussex, BN7 1XU

ISBN 978-1-78494-243-4

All projects previously published in *Woodworking Plans & Projects*, *Woodworking Crafts* and *Furniture & Cabinetmaking* magazines.

While every effort has been made to obtain permission from the copyright holders for all material used in this book, the publishers will be pleased to hear from anyone who has not been appropriately acknowledged and to make the correction in future reprints.

The publishers and author can accept no legal responsibility for any consequences arising from the application of information, advice or instructions given in this publication.

A catalogue record for this book is available from the British Library.

Publisher Jonathan Bailey
Production Manager Jim Bulley
Editor Stephen Haynes
Technical Consultant Alan Goodsell
Managing Art Editor Gilda Pacitti
Design Chloë Alexander
Contributors Amber Bailey, Anthony Bailey, Mark Baker, John Bullar, Fred and Julie Byrne, Walter Hall, James Hatter, Derek Jones, Emma Kennedy, Kevin Ley, Matt Long, Mike Mahoney, Charles Mak, Jim Robinson, Andy Standing
Photography All photographs by the project authors, except for pages 12–13: Emma Noren
Illustrations Simon Rodway

Set in Berthold Akzidenz Grotesk and Rockwell
Colour origination by GMC Reprographics
Printed and bound in Malaysia

A NOTE ON MEASUREMENTS

The imperial measurements in these projects are converted from metric. Though every attempt has been made to ensure that they are sufficiently accurate for practical purposes, some rounding up or down has been inevitable. When following the projects, use either the metric or the imperial units – do not mix the two. If in doubt, make a full-size working drawing before you start cutting.

CONTENTS

INTRODUCTION

None of us has as much leisure as we would like, and woodwork can be a time-consuming occupation. Even if machinery is available to speed up the work, the making of an averagely complex piece of furniture may require a substantial investment of time.

But don't be intimidated: there are plenty of worthwhile woodwork projects that can be accomplished in a weekend (depending on your level of skill and experience, of course), and this book presents more than 30 of them in a clear step-by-step format with measured drawings and helpful photographs. The simplest of them could be made in a couple of hours; others, to be honest, may need a long weekend – but all are accessible to the amateur woodworker who has the basic skills and tools but doesn't have much free time. And of course, as your skills grow, so will the amount of work that you can accomplish in the time you have.

Some of the projects are designed to hone your hand-tool skills, while others rely on that most versatile of hand-held power tools, the router. The authors have often chosen to use machines such as tablesaws and planer-thicknessers, but for those who don't have access to machinery there are always alternatives, from hand-held circular saws to good old handsaws and planes – tools that have been in use for centuries and still, in many circumstances, can't be beaten.

We have also included a few projects that will appeal to those with more specialist interests, such as turning, marquetry and scrollsaw work.

The projects have been grouped by theme: kitchen and dining, home office and study, storage and display, seating, and fun and games. But many of these designs are versatile and you may well prefer to make variations on them rather than copy them just as they are. A rocking chair designed for a teddy bear could be scaled up to fit a child; by changing the proportions of a stool, you could make a bench or a coffee table. And, of course, the choice of materials is always up to you. Feel free to bring your imagination to these projects, and adapt them to your own requirements. Then you can be sure of spending your hard-earned weekends making what you really want to make.

CLASSIC CHOPPING BOARD

There is a special pleasure to be found in making a simple, utilitarian object that will be used and appreciated every day.

The simplest projects often give the greatest pleasure because they don't generally take long to do, and for most people, time is always a bit short. It's also good to use up those odd bits and pieces that oh-so-nearly end up in the woodburner. A nice chopping board goes down well in the kitchen, and makes a perfect present, always well received.

What you need

- Odourless, non-toxic hardwood such as maple or beech
- Plywood or MDF to make the routing jig
- Thicknesser if available (if not, use a jack plane)
- Bandsaw
- Jack plane
- Try-square
- Handsaw or circular saw
- Router with fence, straight cutter, small corebox bit, bevel cutter and ⅛in (3.2mm) roundover cutter
- Hand-held sander, or hand sanding block
- T-square
- Interlocking work support blocks
- Wood file
- Vegetable oil or other food-safe oil

Key
Ø = overall diameter

Plan

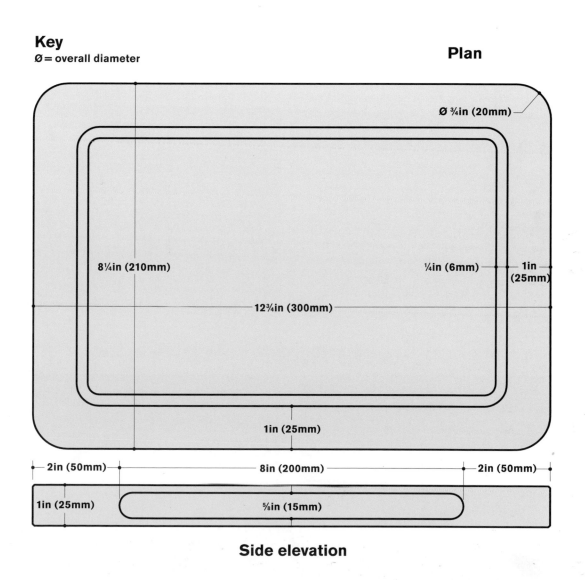

Ø ¾in (20mm)

8¼in (210mm)

¼in (6mm)

1in (25mm)

12¾in (300mm)

1in (25mm)

2in (50mm)

8in (200mm)

2in (50mm)

1in (25mm)

⅝in (15mm)

Side elevation

1 Choose a food-friendly offcut: in this case it happened to be maple (*Acer* sp.), but beech (*Fagus* sp.) or other odourless, non-toxic, light-coloured, tight-grained hardwoods should be suitable. Cut the board oversize and run it down to thickness; here a small thicknessing unit was used, which is perfect for work like this. Make sure both faces are smooth and flat with no snipe (dipped cut) at the ends.

2 Hand-plane the board to width, checking that the edges are square. A jack plane is the correct length for this work.

3 Mark the board ends across with a try-square and pencil the board to length.

4 To cut to length, there are two options. The first is to handsaw it slightly over-length using a good sharp blade…

5 …then use a router, straight cutter and T-square to trim neatly to the marked lines, allowing for the cutter-to-base offset distance.

6 Second method: use a circular saw and the T-square to do a cut to the marked lines. Remember the blade-to-baseplate edge offset. If the cut finish is known from experience to be a bit rough, leave a bit of extra length and use the router to trim.

7 You should now have a nice, neat rectangular board shape. The corners need to be rounded off, so find a suitable shape to draw around – but leave the board square for the moment, to make fenced routing more accurate.

8 Before the corners are shaped we need to make finger-grip slots in the sides to lift the chopping board up by. Make up an L-shaped jig for the router, which is simply two boards screwed together with a bracket underneath to keep it rigid. Make it wider than the chopping board, so the router has support at the start and end of each cut. Drill holes for the screws, to avoid the board puffing or splitting open.

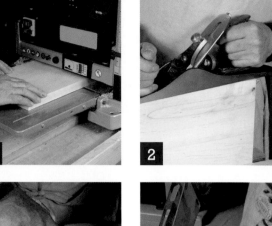

9

10

9 Fix your L-jig in the vice and clamp the board to it, flush with the top of the jig. Mark the slot length about 2in (50mm) short of each end and use the router, fence and a small corebox bit to machine the slots.

10 So long as you control the router by pressing the fence carefully against the jig, you should end up with a nice neat stopped finger recess.

11

12

11 On one side of the board we need a slot to contain meat juices, while the other side is plain for vegetable preparation. To make the slot, use a tiny corebox cutter in the router, working with the straight fence. Here the board is sitting on a set of interlocking support blocks so the fence facing can hang down below the board's edge.

12 Bandsaw off the corners of the board, working close to the line, then use a wood file and abrasives to smooth the shape.

13

14

13 The chopping board edges need a tiny bevel to finish them properly. Make sure the bearing on your bevel cutter doesn't sit too far down, or it will run into the finger recesses and ruin the job. All edges now need a small roundover; use a ⅛in (3.2mm) cutter for a very neat profile. Make sure the cutter isn't set down too low, or the slight step left behind will be hard to remove.

14 Sand fully all over, finishing with fine abrasive. To sand the edges, put the board in the vice before using the sander.

15

15 Use a suitable food-safe finish – the simplest being vegetable oil – and let it soak in. Your board is now ready for the next meal!

NATURAL-EDGE CHOPPING BOARD

These lovely chopping boards are great to use and have a handy hand strap fashioned from leather, neatly secured with mirror screws and caps.

Waney-edged boards have a nice organic feel to them and are perfect for projects such as these simple chopping boards.

What you need

- Waney-edged board of odourless, non-toxic timber such as maple, European sycamore or beech
- Chisel
- Wire brush
- Hand-held sander
- Food-safe finish such as tung oil
- Leather strap
- Mirror screws and caps

1 First, find some offcuts of waney-edged board cut to suitable lengths. Use timbers suitable for food use, such as field maple (*Acer campestre*), European sycamore (*Acer pseudoplatanus*) or beech (*Fagus sylvatica*).

2 Remove all the loose bark with a chisel, taking care not to dig into the wood. Some dark matter may remain, but so long as it is firmly attached, this is OK.

3 A good stiff wire-brushing is next on the menu in order to get rid of any dust, dirt and little creepy-crawlies.

4 Just in case they didn't get the message, the decibels from a sander will soon sort them out. Give both faces a good sanding until you get a smooth but not necessarily even surface.

5 The wood needs to be protected and sealed with a food-safe finish. We chose tung oil, a natural oil that dries and hardens, gives plenty of protection and keeps the wood looking lovely. When dry, use mirror screws and caps to secure the leather strap.

TURNED PLATTER

A simple wooden plate can become part of the history of family life. No other material is more durable and beautiful for the purpose of serving meals.

I have been eating off wooden plates for more than a decade. You can carve a juicy steak; you can serve foods that stain wood and still have useable items. Now, if you can't bear to see your work with knife marks and stains on it, then wooden plates are not for you – but when I see this patina I see history and love, because most of the business of the house is done over the daily meal. The wear and tear are the details of our lives.

Wooden plates must be washed by hand in warm, soapy water and then rinsed. Don't leave them to soak because the wood may swell or crack. Use a soft, clean tea-towel to absorb excess moisture and let the plates finish drying on a draining board. Sanitize wooden plates once a month with a solution of 1 part bleach to 20 parts water.

Making your own dinner plates is relatively easy. The key is to start with a quartersawn piece of wood. Since plates get thoroughly washed daily, they will absorb water then shrink when they dry. Being quartersawn will keep them flat. This makes them easier to use. You will also want to use a wood that is durable for such use. Any soft hardwood that will not taint food will work, such as field maple (*Acer campestre*), European sycamore (*Acer pseudoplatanus*), walnut (*Juglans regia*), the various fruitwoods, beech (*Fagus sylvatica*) and birch (*Betula pendula*). I see a lot of sycamore in the town where I live. Its quartersawn beauty makes it perfect for plates.

Typically, plates average 11in (280mm) in diameter by 1in (25mm) thick. For this particular design I first cut 12 x 1¼in (305 x 32mm) slabs out of the log and sticker them to dry. After approximately 120 days of drying time, I cut the slabs into discs and let them dry for another 120 days. They are then ready to turn.

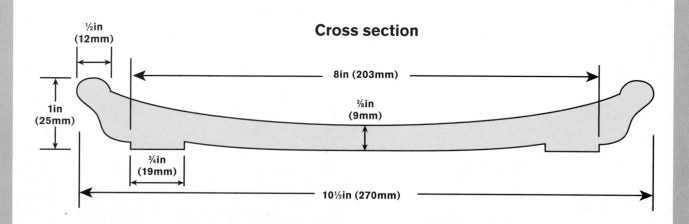

Cross section

½in (12mm)

1in (25mm)

8in (203mm)

⅜in (9mm)

¾in (19mm)

10½in (270mm)

Truing the blank

1 The first step for this project is to mount the plate stock on a screw centre that has a spacer in front of it; this should only let the screw protrude ½in (12mm).

2 Next, you need to secure the stock with the tailstock of the lathe.

3 Now you can true up the diameter, top and bottom of the blank with a ⅝in (16mm) bowl gouge.

Shaping the underside

4 The next step is to remove the tailstock so you can remove wood to form the profile and base.

5 The base diameter for plates should be no smaller than 75% of the total diameter. As this plate is now 10½in (270mm) in diameter, you should mark a base diameter of 8in (200mm).

6 Cut a ³⁄₁₆in (5mm) tenon with a 90° surface to use as a chucking device later on (see photo 12). You can also recess the base a few millimetres to add interest; this will also help stabilize the piece over time.

7 Shear-scrape the profile with a ½in (12mm) shear-scraping bowl gouge.

8 Test with a straightedge to make sure the base will sit flat.

9 Sand to 400 grit, then lightly mist the surface with water to raise the grain and let it dry. Use a worn piece of 400 grit to cut any raised grain, pressing hard at the end to burnish the wood slightly.

Shaping the top

10 Remove the plate from the screw. Make a jam chuck from a 10 x 2in (255 × 50mm) piece of green wood and support this with the screw chuck or any secure means. True it up and mark on it the diameter of the base of the plate.

11 Use a spindle gouge to recess the face of the jam chuck to fit the base of the plate.

12 Cut the recess snugly enough to hold the plate securely while you take cuts from the interior. Do not rely on an insecure fit.

13 Secure the plate in the newly made chuck and support it with the tailstock. Keep the thickness of the plate around ½in (12mm) all over. Address the rim with a ⅜in (10mm) bowl gouge to get the desired thickness, and form a flowing bead shape at the rim with a ⅜in (10mm) spindle gouge to add detail. Don't add any grooves or recesses in which food could lodge.

14 Remove more material in the centre with the ⅝in (16mm) bowl gouge. Remove the tailstock to get full access to the interior surface of the plate.

15 Make a smooth surface, keeping that ½in (12mm) thickness throughout. Sand using the same process as before. Remove the plate by tapping the back of the jam chuck, then sign the piece, add the species of wood and date it. Hopefully your descendants will have a story to tell in the future. Now make a plate for everyone in the house. Better yet, make some for your friends as well.

Since the plate will be getting plenty of use, you should apply a penetrating oil finish rather than a film finish. Film finishes will show wear and will have to be repaired. For this plate a heat-treated walnut oil was used.

MARQUETRY COASTER

Hone your marquetry skills with this arresting trompe-l'œil project, while making a handy place to put your mug.

In the world of design, 'What goes around comes around,' as they say. Houses are becoming filled with vintage, antique and upcycled furniture and furnishings. And the ethos of the cottage crafts industry is finally resurfacing with a desire to relearn traditional skills. Using the age-old decorative technique of marquetry, normally applied to sumptuous antique furniture, this coaster is a classy mix of the traditional with the contemporary, suitably stylish for any coffee table and fitting perfectly into our eclectic lifestyles.

What you need

- At least two photocopies of the paper template (below)
- Two contrasting veneers, one light and one dark
- Scalpel and 10A blade
- Cutting mat
- Veneer hammer
- Pencil
- A means of cutting the groundwork — bandsaw, coping saw or utility knife
- Contact adhesive
- MDF or plywood, 4in (100mm) square by approx. ³⁄₁₆in (5mm) thick
- Sandpaper and sanding block
- Base fabric such as velvet, baize or felt
- Gouache paint and brush
- Superfine white shellac cut with isopropyl alcohol at a 50:50 ratio
- Mop or natural-hair paintbrush
- Fine wire wool
- Cotton cloth
- Light-coloured wax

Template
Actual size

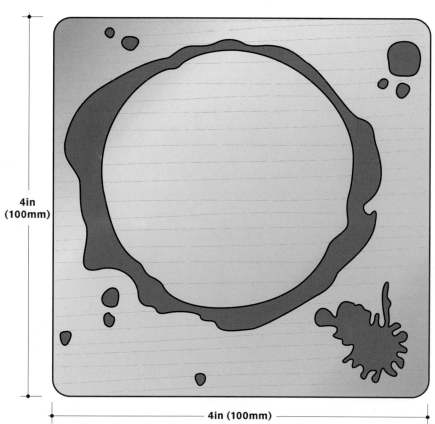

4in (100mm) (vertical)

4in (100mm) (horizontal)

Cutting the marquetry

1 Cut out the spill shape from the first paper template, then overlay this on the light-coloured background veneer.

2 Using a scalpel, cut out this negative space in the light-coloured veneer.

3 Once complete, place the dark veneer underneath and cut out the outer profile of the spill, keeping the circular negative area intact. Both types of veneer should then slot together, and they can be held together with veneer tape on the back to stop pieces from going missing.

4 & 5 Take your second paper template and cut out the central hole of the background veneer. Place this over the marquetry and cut out this shape from the dark veneer. Another piece of the light veneer can then be underlaid and cut out to fit in the gap. Be sure to match the direction of the grain in the two separate pieces of background veneer.

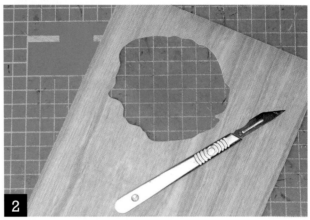

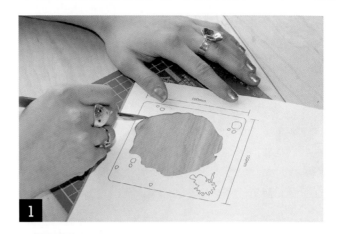

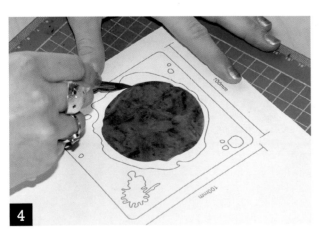

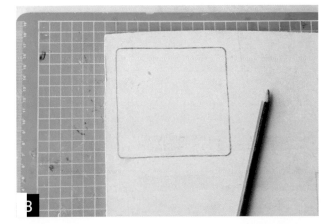

6 & 7 After the main 'spillage' has been cut out, you can then cut out the smaller details using the same method.

Preparing the groundwork

8 The groundwork is the base wood that makes up the core of the coaster; it forms a backing to the marquetry, both to keep it together and to stop it from bowing. With the paper template, draw out the coaster shape onto either MDF or plywood, and then cut out using whichever means you prefer. If you do not have access to a bandsaw or coping saw, then a utility knife will cut through thin MDF, although breaking down the layers is a slow process.

9 Next, smooth down the sides using a sanding block covered in sandpaper, working first with a coarse grade and then a finer one.

Gluing up

10 The marquetry should fit together like a tight jigsaw puzzle, which can then be placed straight onto the groundwork. Using contact adhesive, apply a thin layer to the groundwork and to the back of the marquetry. **Warning:** adequate ventilation is essential when using contact adhesive. Please read the manufacturer's instructions before using.

11 Leave the glue to go tacky then press both pieces together. Rub over with a veneer hammer to flatten the marquetry down and remove any excess glue.

12 When the glue has dried, turn the coaster over and use a scalpel to cut away the excess veneer from the edges.

Smoothing out the surface

13 When the marquetry is complete the surface will not feel smooth, because of differences in the veneer thicknesses. Sand down the surface using a block wrapped in sandpaper, making sure you are always following the grain to avoid scratching the surface unnecessarily. Start with a moderately coarse grade of sandpaper and finish with a finer one to remove the scratches.

Painting the sides

14 Choose a vibrant gouache colour to paint the sides, making sure that it is a complementary colour for the marquetry and the base fabric. Paint the gouache onto the sides of the coaster at quite a thick consistency, but avoid getting any on the marquetry itself. It may take several coats to create a solid colour.

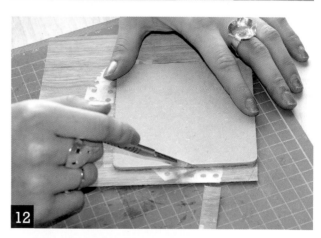

Adding the base fabric

15 The fabric on the base of the coaster will stop it from scratching any furniture surfaces that it may come into contact with. The fabric needs to complement the marquetry and paint as well as being durable enough to take a little wear and tear. Apply a thin layer of contact adhesive to both the back of the fabric and the back of the coaster groundwork.

16 Once the glue has gone tacky, join both sides together and press flat, making sure you remove any excess glue. Remove the spare fabric with a sharp scalpel. If your chosen fabric has a tendency to fray, then apply a thin layer of clear nail varnish around the edges to hold the threads together.

Adding a surface finish

17 To create a glossy finish, use either a polishing mop or a natural-hair paintbrush to apply a solution of superfine white shellac and isopropyl alcohol. Apply the solution in one direction and make sure to avoid drips or brush marks. Leave for a day to harden slightly, then cut back lightly with fine wire wool. Repeat this process several times until you are happy with the gloss level.

18 Once you're happy with the number of layers, apply a light-coloured wax using a piece of cotton cloth. Leave the polish to harden for half an hour, then buff up gently using a clean piece of cloth. This should give your coaster a sleek and silky surface finish.

BUTLER'S TRAY

Whether you have a butler or not, when it's time for 'tiffin' you need a decent tray for those drinks and canapés!

This tray is a standard design but it uses quite a lot of routing. I chose lauan (*Shorea contorta*) for the solid components, as it is slightly pinkish and will colour up easily with dye, and a thin Far Eastern ply for the base, which can be coloured to match. It must be noted that lauan is rather soft and it is not easy to cut crisp jointwork in it.

What you need

- ½in (12mm) hardwood for the sides and ends
- ³⁄₁₆in (4.5mm) plywood for the base
- MDF for the handle template
- Bandsaw
- Router and table with cutters as described in text
- Drill press and Forstner bit, or cordless drill and flat bit
- Half-round metalworking file
- Tenon or dovetail saw
- Chisel
- Sliding bevel
- Double-sided tape
- Aliphatic resin glue
- Wood dye if desired
- Spray lacquer

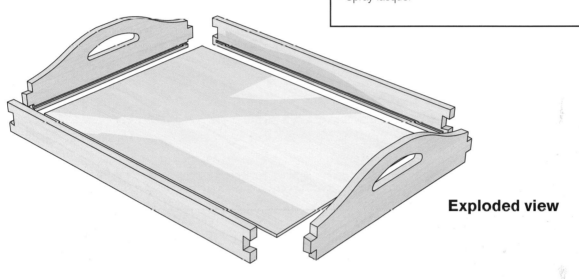

Exploded view

End elevation

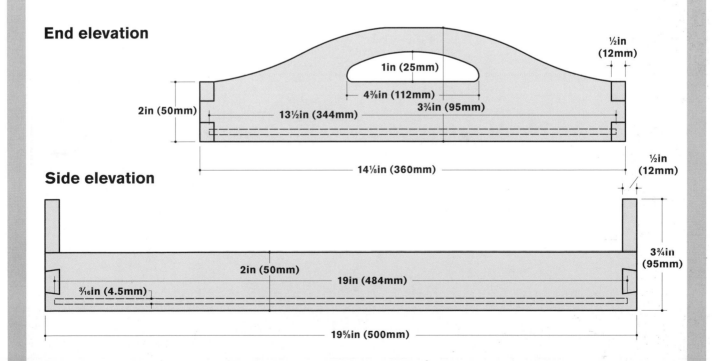

½in (12mm)

1in (25mm)

4⅜in (112mm)

3¾in (95mm)

2in (50mm)

13½in (344mm)

14⅛in (360mm)

½in (12mm)

Side elevation

3¾in (95mm)

2in (50mm)

19in (484mm)

³⁄₁₆in (4.5mm)

19⅝in (500mm)

1 The tray ends need hand grips, and the best way is to make a template that a bottom-bearing-guided straight cutter can run off. Because it is easier to make one half of the shape rather than do both (which may not match), that is exactly what I did. Make the opening big enough to suit larger hands.

2 A standard metalworking file is good to clean the corners. If you want to batch-produce trays, you could use this half-template to make a whole one by cutting it out and turning it over to complete the shape.

3 The finished template is ready to use even though the left-hand side is left rough, as this is the cutter overrun area. It is shaped slightly to mimic the right-hand part of the opening.

4 The template is affixed to one workpiece blank using a special fabric-based double-sided tape which is very adhesive but has a slight sponginess that ensures both surfaces stay fixed together. Take care not to damage the surface when peeling it off. Bandsaw away most of the curved outside edge.

5 I used a drill press and a Forstner bit to remove the bulk of the hand-grip waste. Don't let the bit clip the edge of the template – start with it lower than the template surface, but not touching the wood. You can use a flat bit and cordless drill if a press is not available, but do drill into a sacrificial board to avoid spelching.

6 The next operation is to remove the remainder of the waste using a bottom-bearing-guided straight cutter in the router table. This entails gradually 'grousing out' the waste rather than rushing the cutter straight to the template and taking out too much, straining the cutter and causing too much resistance. Good dust extraction is essential here. During this process I found that the bearing had seized and was burning the wood; fortunately I had a spare.

7 While the template is attached in the same position, repeat the trimming operation on the outside of the hand grip. In both cases, always machine into the direction of cutter rotation and 'downhill' of the grain. Turn the template over and repeat the last three steps to complete the shaping.

8 Using a half-round file, smooth the surfaces so they meet sweetly. Keep the file level to ensure a square edge. For a good surface, push the file diagonally both across and lengthways.

9 The end with the finished hand grip is now attached to the other blank with double-sided tape. As before, bandsaw the outer curve away, leaving enough to trim off on the router table.

10 Using exactly the same procedure as before, the handgrip waste is drilled out ready for profiling.

11 Again 'grouse out' the waste layer by layer; take time over this to get a neat, burn-free result. 'Grousing', my term for widthways removal layer by layer, allows you to sculpt out the waste ready for a final run around the template.

12 Machine the outside of the curve, running 'downhill' of the grain. This is important because if you work towards the top of the hand grip, the wood will tear out. Now lift off and flip over the completed workpiece, tape it down again and machine the other half of the part-completed end.

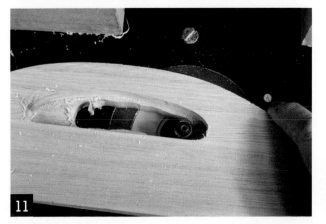

13 You should now have two identical profiled components. Use a small-radius roundover cutter and bearing to shape the top edges. Use a lead-in pin, as you will be starting at the leading end of the workpiece.

14 Now repeat the rounding-over inside the handgrip on both workpieces. This will make the tray comfortable to hold and admit larger hands.

15 The tray sides will be rounded later, as their inside edges require stopped cuts. First, slot all components ready to take the tray base. The ply for this was bought as a ready-cut quarter-sheet with a thickness of just under ³⁄₁₆in (4.5mm). Luckily I happened to have a straight cutter of exactly ³⁄₁₆in (4.8mm), which was close enough. Set the slot in by about ³⁄₈in (10mm), enough not to weaken the wood. Repeated passes will be needed to clear the tightly packed chippings.

16 The sides and ends need to be jointed together and I decided for strength that a single dovetail on the ends would be enough to resist pulling apart. These are marked using a sliding bevel and all the joints should be labelled A, B, C and D to avoid mix-up. Hatch the waste so you cut the right parts away.

17 The first light cut is made vertically to create a notch for the blade to sit in when making the angled cuts. Make clean cuts to the line and finish level at the bottom of each cut.

18 A bandsaw with a 6-skip-tooth blade can be used to cut the waste away, working from each direction until you have a neat level cut along the bottom line. Or you can use a coping saw.

19 Lauan is a rather soft wood, not many stages removed from balsa wood, so a very sharp chisel is required when cleaning up the corner joints. A good but not overtight joint is desirable to avoid any splitting.

20 The dovetailed ends also need a bit of cleaning up for a neat, gap-free fit. Note how the dovetail shape just misses the slot that holds the tray bottom.

21 The tray sides are now rounded over after refitting the cutter; use the table fence this time, not the bearing. Lines are drawn where the roundover needs to run out on the inside edge, then a push-on pull-away cut is made, starting and stopping within the lines, as the outer radius of the cutter will start further along than you may imagine.

22 Sand the flat surfaces thoroughly to a finish on the inside faces, removing any pencil markings. Use a fine abrasive to avoid obvious scratches.

23 Sand all radii thoroughly and blend the curves into the flat sections. Now do a dry assembly to check the bottom size. Cut out the ply and check the fit.

24 Apply glue to the meeting edges of the joints, slide the ply into place and fit all the joints together in the correct order: A–A, B–B and so on. Aliphatic resin glue gives a good, quick bond.

25 Clamp the tray up tightly without creating distortion and measure from corner to corner to ensure squareness. Readjust the clamps to correct any inaccuracy, and wipe off surplus glue.

26 The grooves for the bottom were machined right through, so once the glue has set, remove any glue from the visible slots with a chisel, glue and push in matching fillets of wood and trim these off flush. Finally, sand the outside faces with the grain; avoid cross-grain scratches, as a dark finish will show them up. I swamped the surfaces with a 'Georgian mahogany' spirit dye, wiped off the excess and spray-lacquered the tray once the dye had dried.

TOAST RACK

Not just a handy addition to the breakfast table, this project is also a valuable exercise in the accurate alignment of components.

The answer to most problems in the workshop is to develop a jig that avoids you having to do things more than once, and helps to unify some aspects of the construction. An alignment box jig is a perfect solution for drilling accurate holes in mating components without having to mark out twice. The only critical factor is that it must be square at one corner; the dimensions are up to you.

What you need

- ⅜in (10mm) hardwood of your choice; must be odourless and non-toxic
- Stout MDF to make the box jig
- Bandsaw or jigsaw
- Biscuit joiner and biscuits
- Bobbin sander if available
- Food-safe oil such as tung oil

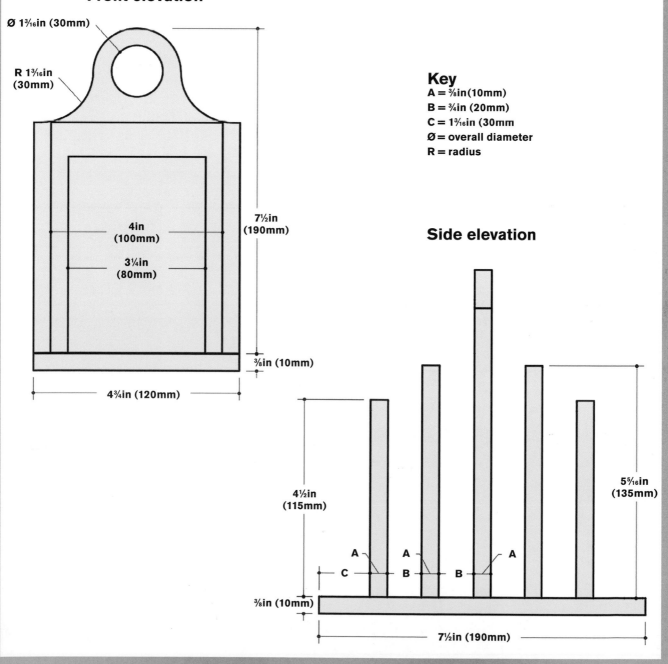

Front elevation

Ø 1³⁄₁₆in (30mm)

R 1³⁄₁₆in (30mm)

4in (100mm)

3¼in (80mm)

7½in (190mm)

⅜in (10mm)

4¾in (120mm)

Key
A = ⅜in (10mm)
B = ¾in (20mm)
C = 1³⁄₁₆in (30mm
Ø = overall diameter
R = radius

Side elevation

4½in (115mm)

5⁵⁄₁₆in (135mm)

A   A   A

C   B   B

⅜in (10mm)

7½in (190mm)

1 I used biscuits to make my box jig, but screws would be quite acceptable. Mark a common edge on the box components for referencing your biscuit slot marks.

2 Assemble the box jig with the edge marks all facing up the same way.

3 When you're satisfied with the box, select the best corner and plant a small fence along two adjacent edges. Ignore the outside edge of the box and concentrate on making sure the inside faces of the two fences are square with the corner edge of the box, and therefore in line with each other.

4 I like to work 'off centres' whenever I can, in the workshop or on site, as this seems to be the most reliable and convenient datum for any number of measurements. Every component has a centre in two axes and, once established, it can be used to simplify cutting, drilling and location. On the underside of the rack, begin by marking centres for the uprights or dividers – in this case, 1³⁄₁₆in (30mm) apart. Extend the lines down both edges and number each line.

5 Take one of the dividers and, with a marking gauge, scribe a line clearly off centre on the bottom edge; then replicate this line from the other face. It should now be simple to find the centre of the piece by eye by positioning the gauge point in the middle of the two marks. Just tap the rod of the gauge on the bench to make tiny adjustments; there is no need to use a ruler. Extend the mark a short way along both sides. At this point the dividers are still the same width as the base of the toast rack.

6 Without a pillar drill, screwing into end grain can prove tricky – but fortunately we have our alignment box jig to get round this. Begin by taking the first divider and clamp it to one side of the jig, tight up to the fence and flush with the top. Now place the baseboard face down on top of the jig, line the marks up on the edge and clamp in place.

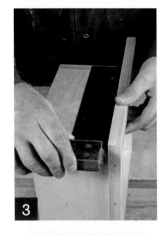

7 Number each centre line and each upright, then drill through the centre line into the divider with a ⁵⁄₆₄in (2mm) bit. To avoid having to mark out an exact position for the holes, just be sure to have the numbers all facing the same way as they are clamped to the jig. Repeat for all the dividers, keeping away from the edges. Re-drill the holes in the base to the gauge of the screws (⅛in [3mm] in this case) and countersink.

8 A simple way to set out the shape on top of the middle divider is to divide the width by four. Take a pair of compasses set to 1³⁄₁₆in (30mm) and mark down from the middle of the top edge to establish a centre for the semicircle. Mark a line across the board and draw the top curve, extending just below the line. Reduce the setting on the compasses by about ¹⁄₃₂in (1mm) and complete the shape either side of the semicircle. You may need to feather the lines freehand to join them up neatly.

9 The shape can be cut using either a bandsaw or a jigsaw. Make a series of straight escape cuts into the curves, stopping just short of the finished line, to let the waste fall away easily and prevent the blade from overheating.

10 A bobbin sander will make light work of smoothing out the curves, but a sheet of abrasive paper wrapped around a thick piece of dowel will work just as well. To finish off, drill a 1³⁄₁₆in (30mm) diameter hole in the centre of the top curve.

11 With all the holes drilled, you can resize the uprights, cutting the same amount of material from each side so that the holes remain central. Now's the time to do any rounding of corners, and sand and finish with a food-safe oil such as tung oil.

12 When putting together, make sure the numbers on the uprights correspond with those on the base in sequence and in orientation.

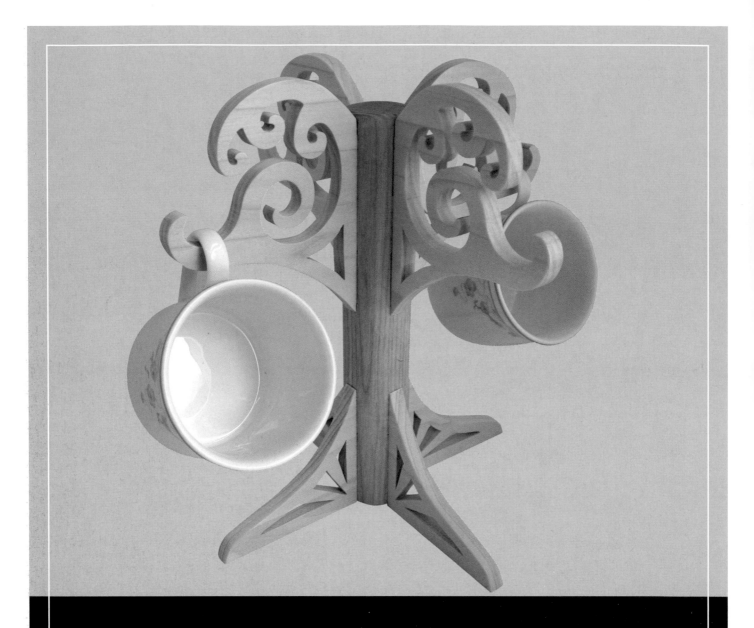

MUG TREE

This simple scrollsaw project will make an attractive, space-saving addition to any kitchen. When space is really at a premium, it might just be the answer you are looking for!

What you need

- 4 pieces of ply @ 4in (100mm) high x 4⅛in (105mm) wide x ½in (12mm) thick for the base brackets
- 4 pieces of ply @ 6in (150mm) high x 4½in (115mm) wide x ½in (12mm) thick for the upper branches
- 1 piece of hardwood @ 9in (230mm) high x 1⅜in (36mm) square for the centre column
- Scrollsaw with No. 9 reverse skip-tooth blade
- Pillar drill with ⁵⁄₃₂in (4mm) bit
- Disc sander
- Traced or photocopied patterns
- Adhesive tape
- Circle template
- Wood glue
- Glue stick or spray adhesive
- Sandpaper: 180, 240 and 320 grits
- Finish of your choice

Any hardwood can be used for the centre column; we used ash (*Fraxinus excelsior*). Two pieces of ¼in (6mm) ash-faced ply were laminated together to make the ½in (12mm) needed for the upper branches and the base brackets. Good-quality plywood has strength in every direction. If you use solid hardwood instead, be very careful about the grain direction in order to have sufficient strength in the hooks.

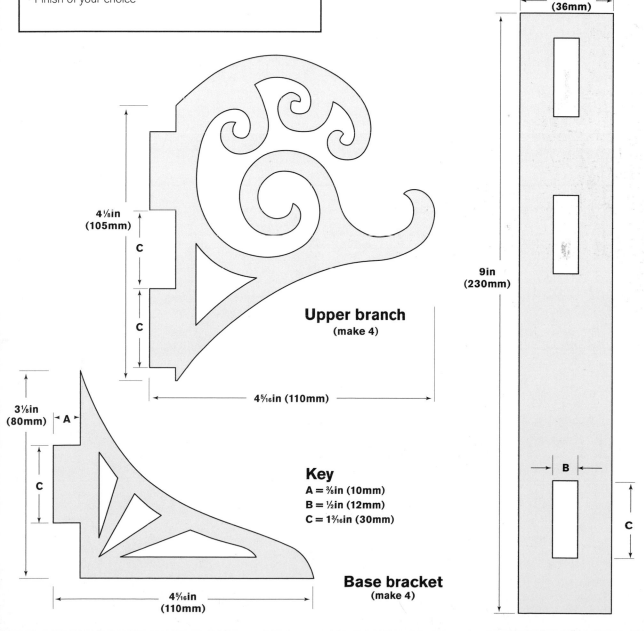

Centre column

1⅜in (36mm)

9in (230mm)

B

C

Upper branch
(make 4)

4⅛in (105mm)

C

C

4⁵⁄₁₆in (110mm)

Key
A = ⅜in (10mm)
B = ½in (12mm)
C = 1³⁄₁₆in (30mm)

3⅛in (80mm)

A

C

Base bracket
(make 4)

4⁵⁄₁₆in (110mm)

1 First you need to make copies of the patterns and then prepare your wood to suit.

2 Cut around the paper patterns, then attach these to the wood with adhesive tape. Tape the pattern for the centre column onto two adjoining sides, and the base and top branch patterns onto the top of each stack of four pieces. If you prefer not to cut stacks of four (giving a thickness of 1⅞in [48mm] in total), then two sets of two would be fine – just make an extra copy of the pattern.

3 Next, fit the pillar drill with a ⁵⁄₃₂in (4mm) bit and drill the blade holes – three in the base, one in the top branch, and six in total on the centre column.

Cutting out

4 Set up the scrollsaw with a No. 9 reverse skip-tooth blade. This has approximately eight teeth going in the opposite direction at one end, which give you a very clean cut with hardly any burr on the underside, and the shape of the teeth makes for a fast cut. As usual in scrollsaw work, do the inner cuts first – this way the stack of pieces stays intact until the last cut. When cutting this thickness of wood, it's important to ensure the blade is set at exactly 90° to the table and that it is very taut, so that blade distortion is kept at a minimum.

5 When making the cuts in the centre column, thread the blade through the central drilled hole as usual and then cut diagonally into each corner.

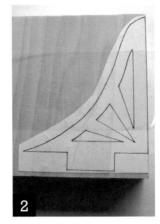

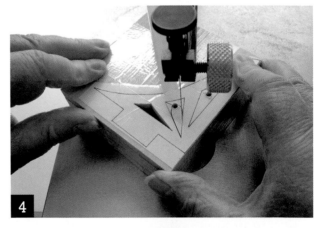

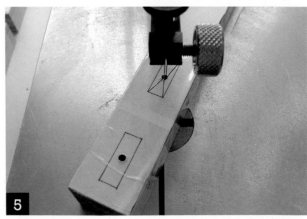

6 Then cut across the ends of the rectangle…

7 …leaving a nice straight run down each side.

8 Once all the enclosed cuts have been made, cut around the perimeters, ensuring that the stack stays intact until the last possible moment.

9 Remove the paper patterns and check the fit of the pieces going into the centre column, making any adjustment that may be necessary.

10 Number each piece and its corresponding location in the centre column; this will be a helpful reference when gluing, especially if you have had to make any adjustments.

Shaping the centre column

11 Mark the position of each base and top branch section of the tree onto the centre column; this will show you where not to sand when rounding off the corners.

12 Use a circle template, or something similar, to mark where to round off the corners at the top and bottom of the column.

13 Using these lines as a guide will help to keep the column symmetrical when sanding.

14 Use a disc sander to round over the edges, being careful not to go beyond your pencil lines.

15 Hand-sand the centre column, going through the grades of paper to remove the scratches left by the disc sander.

16 Use a fine 320-grit sandpaper to remove any burr, and also to round over the edges on the base and top branch pieces.

Finishing off

17 Remove the fine dust from all the pieces and apply a finish of your choice, being careful not to coat where the glue is to be applied, as this will cause problems. Working on a flat surface, lay out the pieces in order of gluing, apply glue to the sections that are to be located into the centre column, and allow each pair a short drying time of approximately 5 minutes or so before turning the column a quarter-turn to glue in the next pair. Continue until all the pieces are in place, then leave to dry fully.

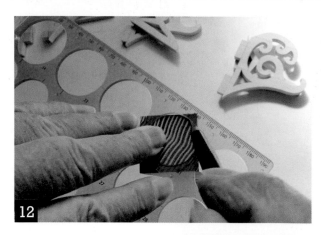

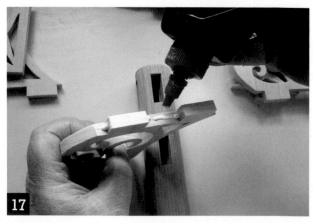

BEER CRATE

It all began with a pile of chuck-out wood that couldn't be used anywhere else. Some of the edges had biscuit slots and grooves, and the wood was narrow so the unwanted machinings couldn't be sawn off. A stackable beer crate proved to be the perfect solution because all these faults became design virtues instead.

Any scrap wood can be used for this project. You might need to try out different bottle shapes and sizes, just to see if they fit the crate design, of course!

What you need

- Scrap wood sufficient to be glued up to the sizes shown in the plans
- MDF or ply for template and housing jig
- Bandsaw
- Jigsaw
- Router with end-bearing-guided straight cutter and roundover cutter
- Random orbital sander
- Glue and clamps
- Shooting board and plane
- Rasp or wood file
- Tenon saw
- Try-square
- Aliphatic resin glue
- Gel stain, or milk paint and sealer
- Abrasives to 120 grit

Plan

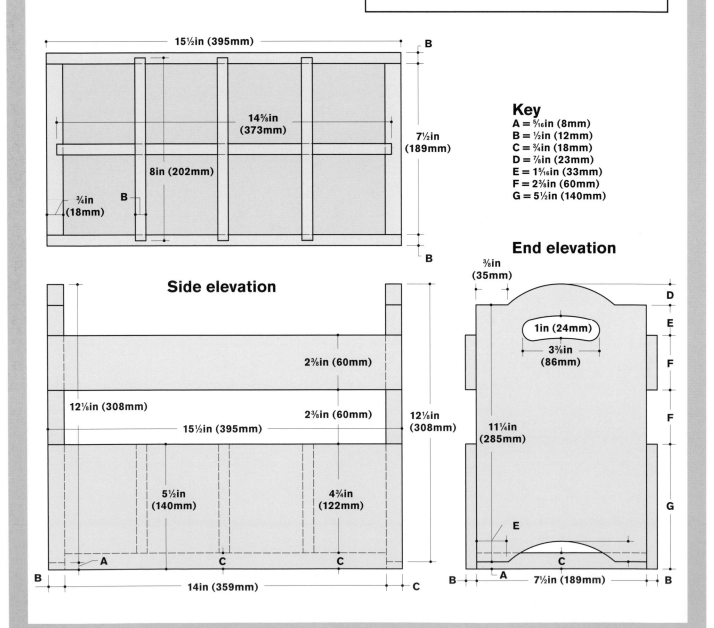

Key
A = ⁵⁄₁₆in (8mm)
B = ½in (12mm)
C = ¾in (18mm)
D = ⅞in (23mm)
E = 1⁵⁄₁₆in (33mm)
F = 2⅜in (60mm)
G = 5½in (140mm)

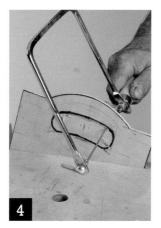

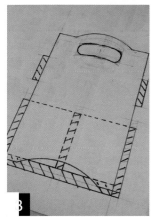

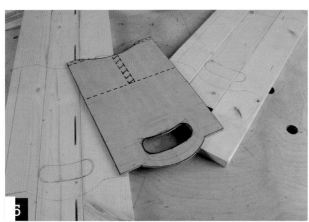

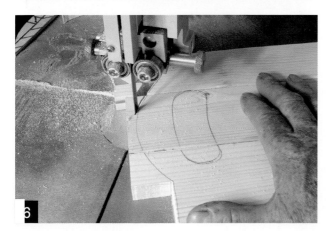

1 The softwood battens were 'ganged' together with glue to make up strips two, three or four pieces wide to suit the design. The widths of the battens were not critical: only the final widths would count.

2 After cutting all the components to length according to the plans, the ends of the boards were all shot by hand to ensure they were nice and square, and checked using a try-square.

3 Having measured up my material, I came up with a 'rod' – a template – which I drew at 1:1 scale. The idea was that the curved ends would interlock if another crate sat on top of the first – but no more than that, for safety's sake.

4 Now the rod became my setting-out and routing template. This involved accurately cutting around the shape of the end (without the side pieces). The edges and hand hole in particular were finely shaped to the drawn line using a hand-stitched rasp with fine teeth, but a coarse wood file will do the same thing.

5 The two crate ends were then drawn out using the template. It wasn't critical to centre the shape on the boards, as the design is supposed to appear deliberately 'flawed', which makes the whole thing more interesting to look at.

6 The crates needed to be cut to identical sizes. The curves were cut on the bandsaw slightly away from the marked line, ready for machining to the finished size.

7 For the hand holes I used a jigsaw, after drilling a blade entry hole. This would later be cleaned up with the router.

8 The template was pinned to each crate end in turn and an end-bearing-guided straight cutter was used to run around the template to create smooth finished edges. Good extraction is essential here. Incidentally, perspective makes my fingers look closer to the cutter than they actually were; this was a safe operation.

9 A roundover was needed on each hand hole for comfort. The cutter needed to be a small enough radius that the bearing would still run along the centre of the board thickness, so the shape didn't get ruined on the second pass from the other face.

10 It didn't even need to be a full roundover – just enough for comfort. A certain crudeness of finish was part of the effect I was after.

11 Now for the bottle partitions. These were carefully marked with a try-square and sawn down to create the halving slots. The boards were thin and apt to break, but holding a tall block against the board while sawing prevented this happening.

12 Once all the cuts were made, the whole assembly could be dry-fitted to see how it went together. Any tight joints could be adjusted by some judicious 'nibbling' on the bandsaw, which helps to widen the slots fractionally.

13 The lower crate sides were marked as a pair where the housings would be machined. The partition boards were just under ½in (12mm) thick and the router cutter exactly ½in (12.7mm) diameter. However, a careful check with digital callipers proved that not all 12.7mm cutters are the same diameter! I ended up choosing the closest one to the actual board thickness.

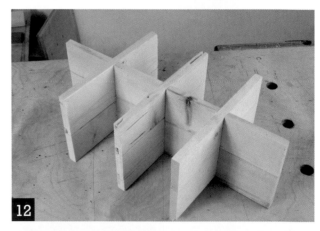

14 I used a housing jig I had made some time ago. It was intended for a ¾in (20mm) guide bush, although you can make a jig to take a smaller one so long as the cutter will pass through easily.

15 To accommodate the bottle partitions I needed a depth of cut of at least ⁹⁄₃₂in (7mm). I chose a ¹⁹⁄₆₄in (7.5mm) drill bit and used the shank of the bit to set the cut depth, an old trick learnt from my colleague Ron Fox.

16 The two crate sides were stacked on top of each other so the housing jig fence batten would sit flat. The jig was then clamped to them and the machining done in two passes until the final depth was reached.

17 However, the crate ends have stopped housings. The same jig was used but a pencil line was drawn on the workpieces as an approximate guide to length.

18 The vital check: will all the compartments fit nicely together? Thankfully, yes.

19 Before glue-up, I checked that the end board was sitting correctly. The curved part needs to be high enough so another crate will interlock underneath it.

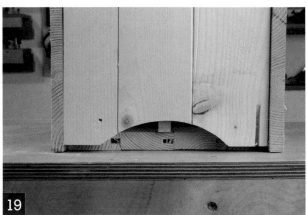

20 The bottle partitions were sanded across the top before assembling the whole crate.

21 All the components were then fitted together with aliphatic resin glue along each housing or butt joint. The bottle partitions didn't need glue as they were pinned to the outside of the crate.

22 They all fit – hooray! Most of the construction was now complete and it was time for a finish to be applied. The top rails were left off to make applying finish to the interior easier to do.

23 First of all, I wanted to experiment with a dark gel stain that would make the crate look traditional. This was a messy job and the stain needed to be wiped off to even it up and allow some wood grain to show.

24 After making that version, I went on to try using milk paints for a completely different 'rubbed-through' effect. The first job was to apply a red milk paint as a base coat with a coat of clear sealer on top of that. I left both coats to dry, then added two coats of a cream-coloured milk paint over that.

25 A combination of 80- and 120-grit abrasives created the rubbed-through effect, which you can see in flea markets, interior design and 'antique' shops everywhere. Easy to do and very effective. Which version you should try is entirely up to you. Have fun!

WINE RACK

This simple but rather eye-catching wine rack relies on the physics of levers, loads and fulcrums. It's not an original concept, but it is rather fun. You can choose whatever shape suits you – the basic principle remains the same.

Precarious though it looks, this rack is perfectly stable provided the centre of gravity of each bottle falls within the footprint of the base; you may need to experiment with the angle of the board in order to achieve this. Many wine experts recommend storing bottles with the neck tilted downwards, as this prevents the cork from drying out and shrinking.

What you need

- ¾in (19mm) timber for the base
- ⅝in (15mm) ply for the board
- Slip of hardwood for the wedge
- Bandsaw
- Tablesaw
- Belt sander
- Random orbital sander
- Router with fence and grooving, dovetail and V-point cutters
- Cordless drill with 1⅜in (35mm) Forstner bit
- Smoothing plane
- Workpiece grippers
- Spray-mount
- Finish of your choice

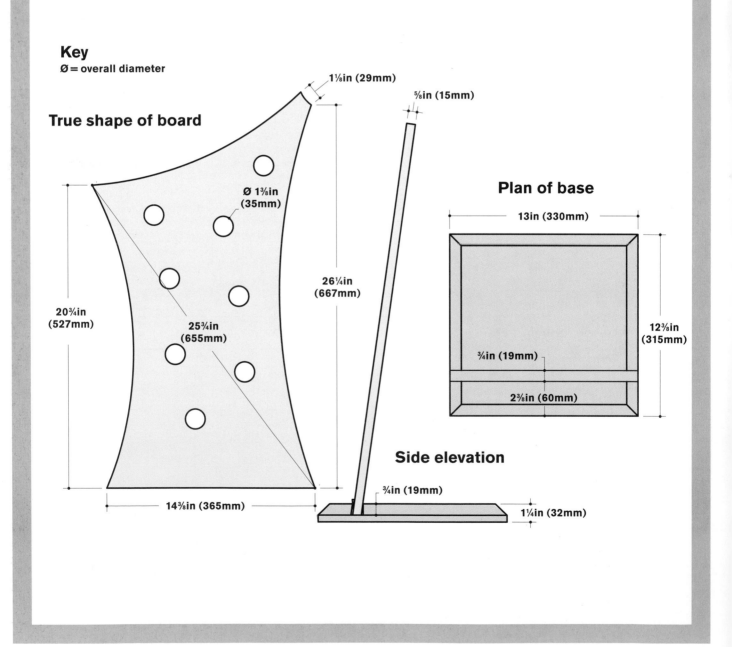

Key
Ø = overall diameter

True shape of board

1⅛in (29mm)

⅝in (15mm)

Ø 1⅜in (35mm)

26¼in (667mm)

Plan of base

13in (330mm)

20¾in (527mm)

25¾in (655mm)

12⅜in (315mm)

¾in (19mm)

2⅜in (60mm)

14⅜in (365mm)

Side elevation

¾in (19mm)

1¼in (32mm)

1 Just two boards are required: a thick piece of softwood or hardwood for the base and an offcut of ply; birch ply is nice and easy to work with. This wine rack will look better with a contrast of timbers. The baseboard needs to be flattened with a belt sander, particularly if you had to glue it up from several sections as I did. I worked cross-grain, planning to eradicate the scratches with an orbital sander afterwards.

2 The slot for the board holding the bottles needs to be about 2⅜in (60mm) from one of the end-grain edges – far enough to prevent the applied weight of the bottles from causing breakout. This slot should run across the grain for the same reason.

3 A straight slot, wider than the thickness of the angled board, is cut with the router, making a number of passes to reach the required depth. Really good control is needed to prevent the router wandering off course. The slot should go slightly deeper than half the baseboard thickness.

4 A test fit shows whether the angle is roughly correct. However, the board won't fit snugly at this stage and it will need to angle a bit more. By improving the fit it will look better and be more secure.

5 I fitted together a group of these workpiece grippers to rest the baseboard on for the next operation, as I needed to use a large router and a fence that would not drag on the bench top.

6 Here I am using a large dovetail cutter to angle the slot on the side closest to the baseboard edge.

7 The finished slot. The added angle will allow the board to sit more neatly. The breakout at the front edge doesn't matter as it will be machined away later.

8 The bottom edge of the angled board needs to be bevelled so it sits flat on the bottom of the baseboard slot. I have finally got around to using my antique Sargent No. 4½ smoothing plane; its handling and blade sharpness are not bad for a restored late-Victorian hand tool!

9 The fit has improved. Since the weight of the bottles will hold the rack together, I decided not to fill the gap behind the angled board. You can see how much force eight or so wine bottles could confer on this rather vital 'junction', rather than 'joint'.

10 A large V-point cutter on a ½in (13mm) shank is used to create a wide bevel on the top edges of the baseboard. I wanted an impressive 'tablet' effect. Make a number of passes to achieve the final depth. This operation will remove the tearout noted earlier.

11 This is a good point at which to sand and finish the base before working on the angled board. Any suitable clear finish will do. At least one coat is needed so it is protected from marking; more coats can be applied later.

12 My inspiration for the shape, without wishing to sound pretentious, came from Salvador Dalí and from the cartoon styles of the Fifties – a sort of asymmetric shape that defies straight-and-square. I designed it with some simple pencil strokes.

13 Even at the bandsaw stage I didn't slavishly follow my drawn lines, because I wanted quickly formed even curves that wouldn't need a lot of cleaning up afterwards. I moved the board as quickly as I could without stalling the bandsaw.

14 I drew some bottle apertures on the board to give me an idea of how many bottles and what positions were required. In the end I drilled wherever it seemed right and rather ignored my own sketching out.

15 Before going any further I did some experiments to see how well a bottle neck would sit in a hole. I found that a 1⅜in (35mm) Forstner bit used freehand in a cordless drill produced the perfect hole size for standard wine bottles. I then tried a routed roundover to help the neck fit in better, but it didn't work as it wouldn't hold the bottle so well.

16

17

18

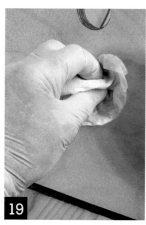

19

16 Although I drilled into a sacrificial board, the ply face tended to break out around the holes. To overcome this I spray-mounted ordinary copier paper on the underside before drilling, rubbing it down firmly. This seems to hold the wood fibres together as the bit breaks through.

17 I decided to use a tiny bevel on both faces around the edges of the bottle apertures for the sake of tidiness. At this point the board needs to be sanded to a finish; break the arrises (that is, soften the sharp edges where the front and back of the board meet the edge of it) but don't sand the actual edges, as the fine-tooth bandsawn finish is adequate.

18 I experimented with bottles and decided that the angled board sat better when it rested against the back of the slot, as the centre of balance then moved slightly also. I cut a very slim wedge of walnut (*Juglans regia*) on the tablesaw, tapped it into the slit with some glue and left it proud for effect.

19 Once the rack is assembled, it is time for a final coat of finish. I used my favourite wax oil which gives a golden appearance. Don't forget to lay out used pads or rags to dry away from everything and thus avoid any fire risk.

20 Now you can display your wine bottles in an interesting way, rather than hiding them away in a cupboard to gather dust!

20

ROUBO BOOKSTAND

If you enjoy projects that challenge your hand skills to the limit, a Roubo bookstand is a good choice. This hinge-like bookstand, made from a single piece of wood, is as functional as it is intriguing. It was first described in print in 1769 by the French joiner and cabinetmaker André Jacob Roubo, though more ornamental versions have been used in Muslim countries since the 13th century.

For this project, I chose an American cherry (*Prunus serotina*) board, with a hinge design consisting of five joint sections. In essence, the construction involves laying out the hinge, cutting out the hinge joints, forming the edge profiles and, finally, sawing the board in half to make a foldable stand.

What you need

- Hardwood board, approx. ¾ x 5⅛ x 13in (20 x 130 x 330mm) (dimensions may be varied to suit individual requirements)
- Combination square
- Marking knife
- Chisel, preferably the same width as the hinge knuckle
- 45° bevel gauge, home-made from plastic card
- Fretsaw
- Pliers
- Backsaw
- Panel saw
- Smoothing plane
- Cabinet scraper
- Spokeshave if needed
- Coping saw if needed
- Rasp and/or file as needed

Front elevation (folded)

Side elevation (folded)

Bookstand unfolded

This diagram shows an alternative method of starting the saw kerf when sawing the board in half. Clamp a saw blade down on a scrap spacer block that elevates the saw teeth to the centre line of the board. Simply run the board back and forth on the bench against the saw teeth until you have established a deep guiding kerf.

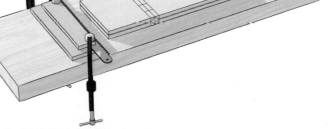

Timber selection

Choose a board of a size suitable for the books you intend to use with the bookstand. For this project, I chose an American cherry (*Prunus serotina*) board about ¾ x 5⅛ x 13in (20 x 130 x 330mm), with a hinge design consisting of five joint sections.

Laying out the hinge

1 Locate the hinge centre line on the board, usually at one-third of the length of the stock. Extend this centre line around all four faces of the board.

2 On both edges of the board, draw a diamond shape centred on this line; this will be used in the next step to define the hinge boundary lines.

3 Extend the points of the diamond around the board on all faces. Holding the square in the manner shown ensures precision when scribing or marking a line.

4 Divide the width of the board into the desired number of sections (five in this case) and scribe or mark the dividing lines with a marking knife – a combination square can be used like a stop rule, as shown. Repeat the marking process on the back of the board.

5 Starting with the top left box on one face of the board, shade the alternating rectangles. Then flip the board over end to end and again shade alternate rectangles starting at the top left. Mark out clearly the direction of each sloping cut, chopping from the centre line down towards the hinge boundary line – and remember that no vertical cuts are made on any hinge centre line.

Here are a few suggestions to make the chopping more accurate:
- Use a chisel sharpened at 30° or higher.
- Choose a wide chisel over a narrow one where possible.
- Make a bevel gauge (a right-angled isosceles triangle) from a plastic card to check the progress of the work.
- Wrap masking tape around the chisel to serve as a depth gauge at half the thickness of the board.

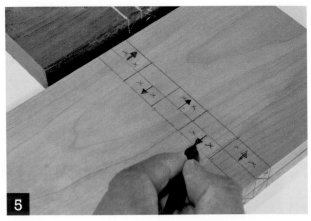

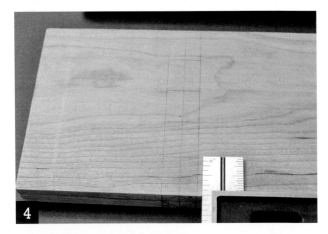

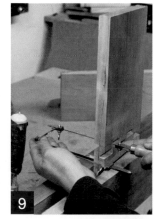

6 Begin the vertical chopping a little way in from the scribed boundary line.

7 When making the initial sloping cuts, place a combination square alongside or use the bevel gauge to help orient the chisel at 45°.

8 Check the cuts with the bevel gauge as you chisel away the waste. A depth mark drawn on the gauge will avoid overcutting. Make the final vertical cut right on the scribe line, stopping at half the thickness of the board, and clean up the bevel with paring cuts. After all the bevels are cut on one face, flip the board over and repeat the process.

9 Use a fretsaw to separate the walls between the hinge sections (or you may choose to saw the walls before chopping out the sections; either method works well). Drill blade-entry holes at the tops of the dividing lines and saw the long grain between the sections.

10 If your fretsaw's throat is not long enough to reach, use pliers to bend the blade at 90° so you can hold the saw handle horizontally.

Splitting the board

11 Resawing the board evenly down the length can be quite a challenge, especially in wide and long hardwood. The trick is to form a true kerf on the edges to guide the sawing. First, mark a centre line around the four edges; I actually prefer to lay out two lines, about the thickness of a saw kerf apart, to guide the ripping. You can start and finish the sawing with a panel saw, but for narrower stands I usually begin with a backsaw for better control, approaching the job as if I were cutting a tenon.

12 Tilt and clamp the board in a vice so you can see the layout lines on both edges to cut straight and square. Rest the backsaw with its teeth between the lines and make cuts across the far corner and gradually down the centre lines on the top edge. Then angle and run the saw down on the edge nearest you until you reach about an inch (25mm) deep, forming a starter kerf.

13 Once the kerf is formed, switch to a panel saw and saw down to the hinge boundary line. If the saw binds, wax the blade and use a wedge to keep the kerf open. Repeat the sawing from the other end. Carefully open up the hinge; if the pieces do not open, examine and remove any uncut fibres along the stop cuts or hinge sections. Once separated, cut the front half to length to form the ledge or book rest. Clean up the hinge with a chisel and remove the saw marks on the board with a small plane and a cabinet scraper.

Shaping the ends

14 Lay out your chosen profiles and cut them out with backsaw, spokeshave, fretsaw or coping saw as applicable. If using a fretsaw, install the blade to cut on the pull stroke, so if it snaps, your fingers are not in the way.

15 Finish the shaping with rasps, files or scrapers. After signing the work, I applied coats of boiled linseed oil as well as a coat of beeswax to the stand. If you prefer a darker look, expose the surfaces to sunlight for several hours before finishing the stand with oil and wax.

Here are some alternative designs in different timbers. A hand-cut and hand-rubbed Roubo bookstand has a touch of elegance that other bookstands just don't have. It definitely brings something extra to the reading experience, whether you have a traditional book or an e-book reader on the stand.

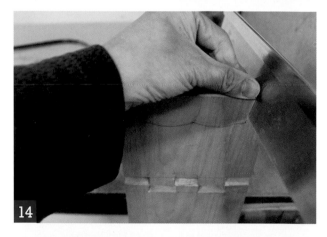

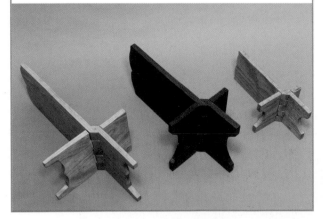

OFFICE SHELF

A shelf to hold box files needs to be rather substantial, but can still be stylish. The Art Deco-style cutouts in this design give it a sense of lightness despite its size and solidity.

The wood chosen for this project is American cherry (*Prunus serotina*). This usually comes in lengths of about 7ft (just over 2m) and in fairly narrow widths, so some edge-jointing to make up the width required for the ends and shelves is inevitable. The boards often incorporate sapwood, so a decision has to be made whether to remove all the sapwood or to retain it as a feature.

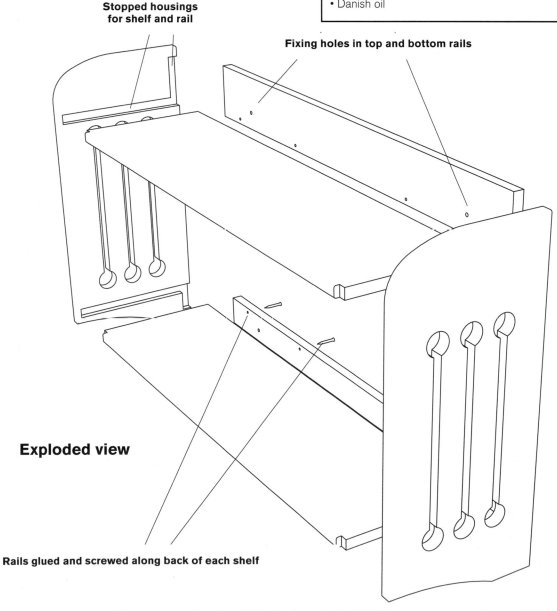

Stopped housings for shelf and rail

Fixing holes in top and bottom rails

Exploded view

Rails glued and screwed along back of each shelf

Split front elevation

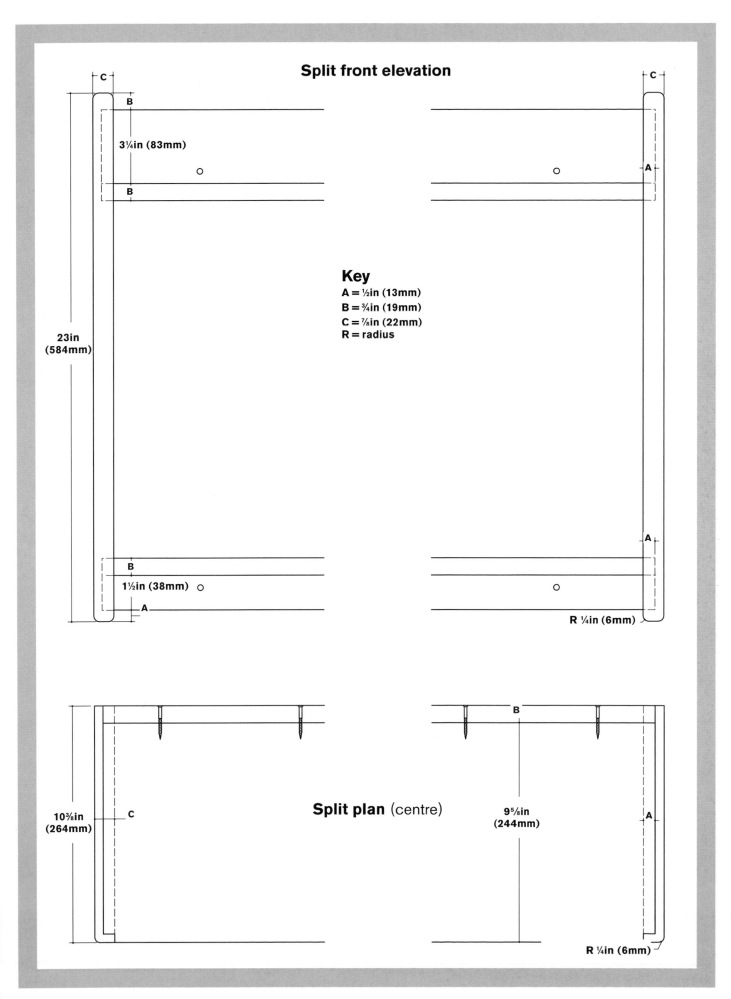

3¼in (83mm)

23in
(584mm)

1½in (38mm)

Key
A = ½in (13mm)
B = ¾in (19mm)
C = ⅞in (22mm)
R = radius

R ¼in (6mm)

Split plan (centre)

10⅜in
(264mm)

9⅝in
(244mm)

R ¼in (6mm)

Front elevation

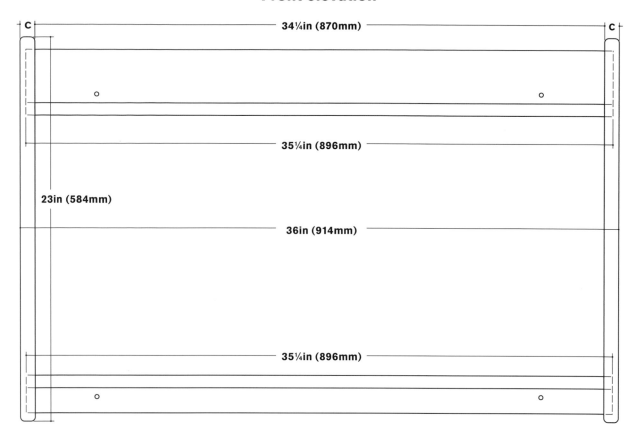

34¼in (870mm)

C | C

35¼in (896mm)

23in (584mm)

36in (914mm)

35¼in (896mm)

Key

A = ½in (13mm)
B = ¾in (19mm)
C = ⅞in (22mm)

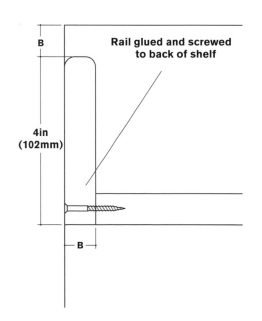

B

Rail glued and screwed to back of shelf

4in (102mm)

B

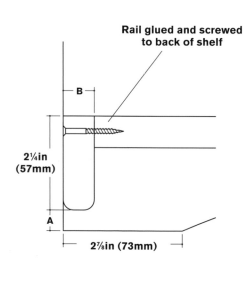

Rail glued and screwed to back of shelf

B

2¼in (57mm)

A

2⅞in (73mm)

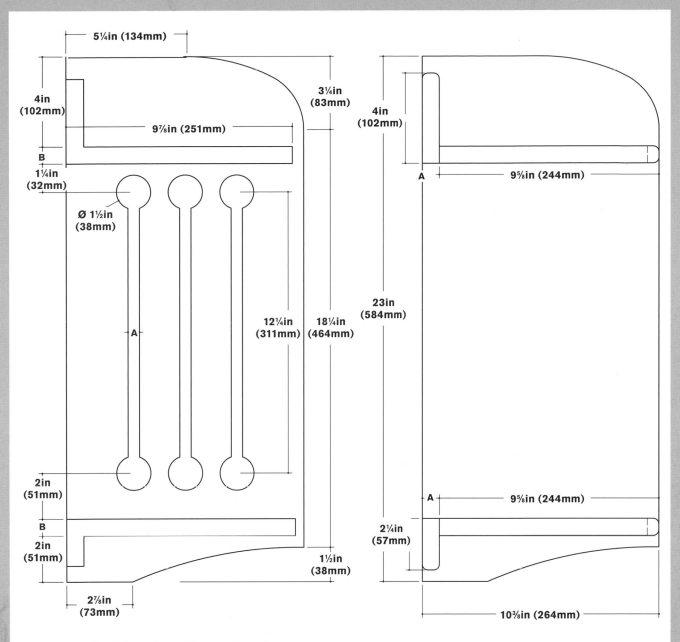

Inside elevation of end

Key
A = ½in (13mm)
B = ¾in (19mm)
Ø = overall diameter

Cutting list

Ends	2 @ 23 x 10⅜ x ⅞in (584 x 264 x 22mm)
Shelves	2 @ 35¼ x 9⅝ x ¾in (896 x 244 x 19mm)
Upper rail	1 @ 35¼ x 4 x ¾in (896 x 102 x 19mm)
Lower rail	1 @ 35¼ x 2¼ x ¾in (896 x 57 x 19mm)

Preparation

1 The first step is to saw the boards into suitable lengths to make up the ends and the two shelves. Then plane one side of each board flat.

2 Now pass through a thicknesser to give you the required thickness.

3 Plane the edges of the boards to be joined so that they are straight and square, ready for gluing.

4 A simple glue joint is sufficient to join the boards. Biscuits are not necessary because the joints will be reinforced when the shelves enter the housings cut in the ends. I prefer to use a synthetic powdered resin glue rather than a PVA type, as PVA is heat-sensitive and can spread when sanding. The boards should be held in clamps until set, and any surplus glue that squeezes out is best removed when the glue is at the rubbery stage, with a spatula or an old chisel.

5 Use a belt sander to level the boards and remove all traces of glue.

Making the ends

6 Mark out the shape of the ends and the positions for the shelf housings and the decorative openings. Use a French curve if you're not comfortable with drawing freehand.

7 Mark out the centres of all the large holes with a bradawl. The holes are 1½in (38mm) in diameter. I used a machine sawtooth bit (similar to a Forstner bit) to sink them, using a drill press. Make sure your drill press has enough width between pillar and drill bit; otherwise it will be necessary to drill the holes before gluing the wood together to make up the width. Start by drilling a small-diameter hole through the timber at each hole position, so that you have a pilot hole on each side of the wood in which to locate the centre point of the large bit.

8 Locating the sawtooth bit in the pilot hole, drill a little over halfway through from one side, then turn the board over to complete the hole from the other side.

9 The sawtooth bit produces a particularly clean hole. If you do not possess a drill press but do have a lathe, you could mount a chuck in the headstock and a faceplate in the tailstock to form a horizontal bench drill. Drilling this size of hole cleanly with a hand-held power drill is not easy, but you could use a brace with a 1½in (38mm) diameter auger. If you try using a spade bit in a power drill, you will be very lucky if the two sides meet exactly. The holes drilled may need a little sanding before proceeding to the next stage, which is cutting the slots between the holes.

10 Using a ½in (12.7mm) diameter cutter in a hand-held router guided by a fence, sink a rebate about halfway through the thickness before turning the wood over and completing the slot from the other side. The two outer slots are best worked from their nearest side – provided, of course, that the opposite edges of the board are exactly parallel. This avoids having to use long guide bars on the fence, which make it a little harder to avoid any wobble during the cut. The central slot can be guided from either side.

11 The next stage is to form the stopped housings for the shelves. Clamp a batten in the correct position to guide the router fitted with a ¾in (19mm) straight cutter; the clamps used to hold the batten also serve to hold the workpiece securely to the bench. Take out the housings in two or three passes to a depth of ½in (13mm), and be careful to finish short of the ends.

12 The upstand or rail at the top of the shelf and the support rail below the bottom shelf will be glued and screwed to the rear edge of the shelves. To accommodate these, sink a small housing in the inside face of each end using the same router cutter, but this time guided by a fence fixed to the router. These housings are stopped short and the ends squared by hand with a chisel.

13Cut the top and bottom edges of the end pieces square, then complete the shaping on the bandsaw.

14A belt sander removes all teeth marks.

15Sand all faces and edges smooth, then use a hand-held router fitted with a ¼in (6.4mm) radius self-guided cutter to round over the external edges.

The shelves

16Plane and glue the boards to the required width, as you did for the ends. American cherry is usually only available in boards not much more than 5–6in (125–150mm) wide.

17Hold the shelves in clamps until set, then cut to size and sand smooth. Work an ⅛in (3.2mm) radius along the front edges with a router and bearing-guided cutter.

13

14

15

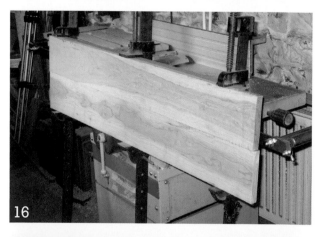

16

17

18 Place the shelves in their housings and then mark the small cutout required at the front corners: this can be most effectively achieved using a flat marking knife resting against the surface of the uprights. Make the cutout with a fine-toothed saw. Note that the shelves finish ¾in (19mm) short of the back in order to allow for the thickness of the longitudinal rails. The rails will be glued and screwed to the back edges of the shelves, entering the housings created to receive them at the ends.

19 Before gluing, give the whole thing a really good sanding through the grits; this is much easier done before assembly. A palm sander speeds the work.

20 When gluing the shelves to the ends, I used a PVA glue and applied it to the housings only, so the shelves pushed the surplus in rather than out, thus making very little to clean up. Now clamp it up and leave to dry.

21 Drill and countersink two holes in each rail for fixing to the wall.

22 The shelf unit was finished by applying a sealing coat of Danish oil with a brush; after a few minutes any surplus remaining was removed with a lint-free cloth. The finish was applied to the ends before doing the shelves and back. Allow the shelves to dry fully for a few days before applying a coat of clear wax polish and buffing up ready for fixing in position. All you need to do now is to hope the wall surface is flat!

DESK SET

Transform a collection of oddments and leftovers into a businesslike set of matching desk accessories: filing trays, pen holder and letter rack.

What you need

- Oak and plywood per cutting list
- Tablesaw
- Bandsaw
- Belt sander
- Router table and straight or rebate cutter
- Band clamp
- Drill
- Screwdriver and screws
- Glue
- Panel pins and hammer
- Mitre square
- Abrasive paper

Cutting list

All parts oak (*Quercus* sp.) except as stated

Filing tray (materials for one)
Sides   2 @ 12½ x 2 x ⁵⁄₁₆in (320 x 50 x 8mm)
Ends   2 @ 9½ x 2 x ⁵⁄₁₆in (242 x 50 x 8mm)
Base (ply)   1 @ 12½ x 9½ x ⁵⁄₁₆in (320 x 242 x 4mm)

Pen stand
Base   1 @ 6 x 4 x ¾in (150 x 100 x 20mm)
Upright   1 @ 3½ x 4 x ¾in (90 x 100 x 20mm)

Letter rack
Base   1 @ 10¼ x 4 x ¾in (260 x 100 x 20mm)
Rear support 1 @ 9½ x 4 x ¾in (242 x 100 x 20mm)
Front bar   1 @ 9½ x 4 x ¾in (242 x 40 x 20mm)

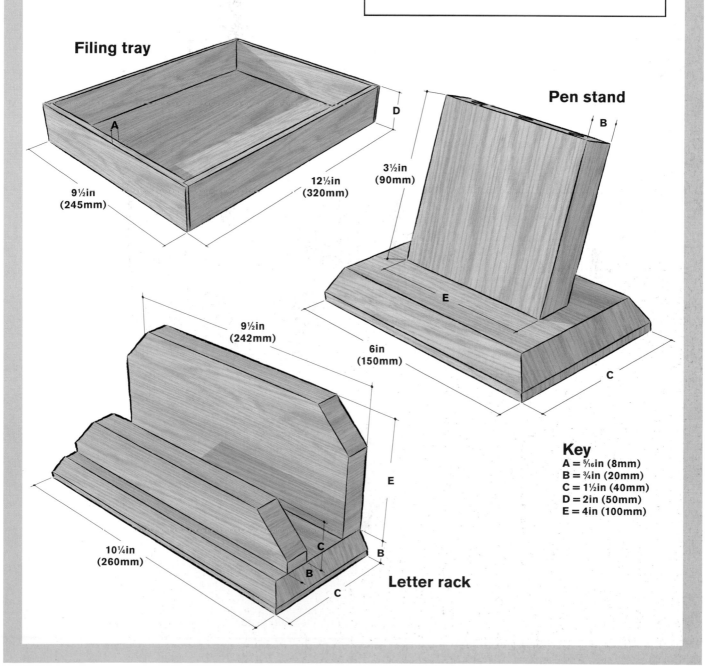

Filing tray

9½in
(245mm)

12½in
(320mm)

D

Pen stand

B

3½in
(90mm)

E

6in
(150mm)

C

9½in
(242mm)

E

10¼in
(260mm)

C

B

C

B

Letter rack

Key
A = ⁵⁄₁₆in (8mm)
B = ¾in (20mm)
C = 1½in (40mm)
D = 2in (50mm)
E = 4in (100mm)

Making the trays

1 You are bound to have some scraps lying around the workshop that can be put to good use. I started with these short oak boards and a rather nondescript piece of ply. Because the timber I had was ¾in (20mm) thick, it had to be resawn on the bandsaw down to ⁵⁄₁₆in (8mm) to make the sides for the filing trays.

2 Next, clean up the sawn faces with a belt sander.

3 Now you can rip the pieces to width using a tablesaw…

4 …and then crosscut them to the correct length.

5 The plywood base of the tray will sit in a rebate cut into the sides. To set the depth of the rebate, take a scrap of the ply base and use it to set the cutter height on your router table. Set the cutter protrusion so that it is about two-thirds of the thickness of the sides.

6 Standing the side components vertically against the fence, cut the rebates on their bottom edges. Use featherboards and a push stick to keep your hands well away from the revolving cutter.

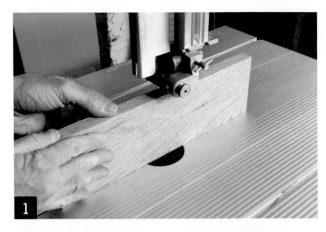

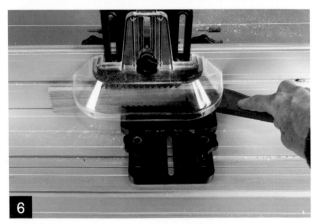

7 The corners of the tray are joined using lap joints, cut on the router table. Set the cutter protrusion so that it is fractionally more than the thickness of the timber and set the cutter height so that it lines up with the edge of the rebate when the timber is laid on its side.

8 As you are cutting across the end grain of the sides, you must use a mitre fence with a timber support board behind the workpiece. Cut the joints in both end pieces.

9 Once the joints are cut, assemble the frame – without glue for now – and support it with a band clamp. Note the small overlaps on the corners, which you will be sanding off after assembly for a nice neat finish.

10 Measure the inside of the rebate and cut your piece of plywood to fit. Cut it a little oversize to start with and then take shaving cuts until you have an exact fit.

11 A perfect fit. Now dismantle the frame and reassemble using glue. Glue the base panel in place and insert a few panel pins if you like. Set the tray aside and leave the glue to cure.

12 Finally, carefully go over the piece with some fine abrasive paper to remove any sharp edges and leave the surface smooth to the touch.

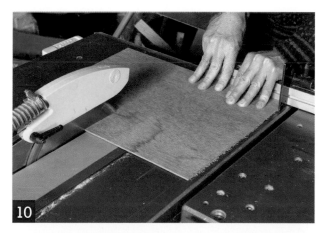

Bevelled edges

The pen stand and the letter rack both have bases with a bevelled edge. You can machine this on the router table, or alternatively you can use the tablesaw. First cut the bases to size, then tilt the blade to 30° and trim the edges, using the rip fence to guide you. The pen stand has all four edges bevelled, but the letter rack only has the two ends and the front edge bevelled; the rear is square.

The pen stand

13 The pen stand is a short length of board with three or more holes bored in the end to hold the pens. Use a ½in (12mm) diameter drill mounted in a pillar drill to ensure that the holes are drilled straight and your pens won't stand at a slant.

14 The board is mounted on the base at an angle – 20° off vertical is about right – so tilt the saw blade by that amount and crosscut the end of the board.

15 Mark the centre line across the baseplate.

16 Next, drill a pair of holes to suit the width of the board, making sure they don't clash with the pen holes.

17 Hold the board vertically in a vice and attach the baseplate with a pair of screws.

18 Your completed pen holder should look like this.

The letter rack

19 The letter rack has three components: the baseplate, the rear support and the front bar. To harmonize with the bevelled base, the corners of the rear support and the front bar are removed, though rather than using the 30° angle, a 45° slope looks better here. Mark both components using a mitre square.

20 Using the mitre fence on your tablesaw, or using a handsaw, make the cuts on the rear support…

21 …and then do the same for the front bar.

22 The components are simply screwed together. Mark their positions on the top of the base and drill holes for the screws. The rear support is fixed flush with the rear of the base; the front bar is set back about ⅜in (10mm) from the front.

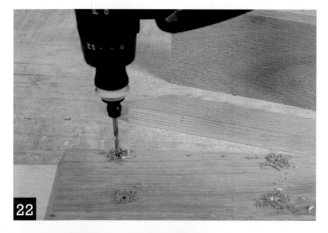

23 Fit the rear support first, then clamp the front bar in place and invert the rack while you screw it in position.

24 Here is the completed rack, ready for use.

LETTER RACK
WITH DRAWER

This three-part letter rack, complete with a neat little stationery drawer, is the perfect way to keep the clutter on your desk or hall table under control.

This project uses ¹⁄₂in and ¹⁄₄in (12mm and 6mm) veneered ply or MDF, with the edges left raw as they can be stained down to a more acceptable colour. Although my letter rack sits on a table, it could just as well be wall-mounted instead.

11in (278mm)

8⅝in (220mm)

2⅜in (61mm)

B   **10½in (266mm)**   **B**

Front elevation

Key

A = ¹⁄₄in (6mm)
B = ¹⁄₂in (12mm)
C = 2⁵⁄₁₆in (59mm)
D = 2⁷⁄₈in (73mm)
E = 3in (76mm)
F = 4¹⁄₈in (104mm)
G = 5¹⁄₈in (130mm)

E

E

8⅝in (220mm)

E

G

B   **B**

F

D

A

C

5¾in (147mm)

Cross section

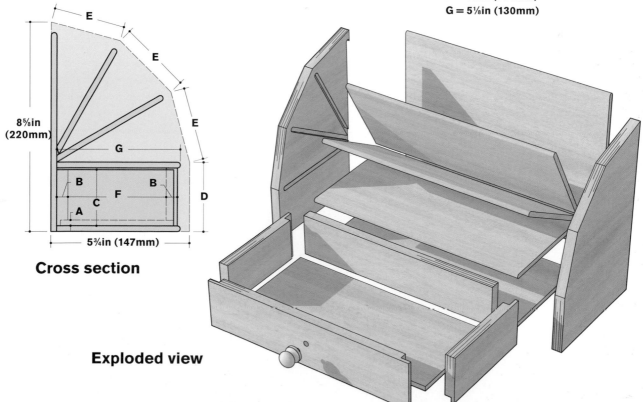

Exploded view

1 The first step is to make a template of the end profile. Once drawn, it will then be used to machine the slots needed. Use ¼in (6mm) MDF; this should be thick enough for most guide bushes without them protruding.

2 The template is temporarily spray-mounted to a suitable board. I use offcuts of polyurethane insulation board, as it offers minimal resistance to cutters. I often find pieces in builders' skips. A fillet is then pinned on to act as a fence for the router, which has a ½in (12mm) straight cutter fitted. Each slot is then machined right through the MDF. Make sure the slots do not run right through to the front edge of the rack end!

3 Note how the fillet position changes in order to create each slot; you may need to change the locations of the pins so they always fix into the MDF. Care is needed to create even slots that meet together nicely.

4 The outer slots are not strictly slots but rebates, as they are open-sided. It will be easier to line the template up with the workpiece if both uncut sections of edge meet. A waste piece of MDF acts as 'land' for the other side of the router to rest on.

5 Now use carpet tape or special-purpose narrow jig tape to stick the template to the workpiece.

6 A ½in (12mm) guide bush combined with a ¼in (6.4mm) straight cutter is used to machine the divider slots in one of the rack ends. (Do not use a larger guide bush, or the large cutter needed to create the slots will ruin the template.) The template is then removed and turned over to create the other slotted rack end.

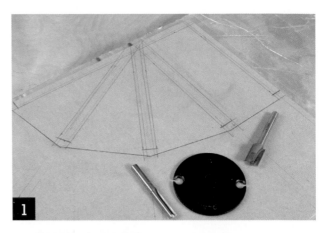

7 The ½in (12mm) ply, showing both sets of slots. The next job is to cut out the shapes of the end pieces.

8 Cut out the front edge shape on the template and clean the edges to the drawn line. I used a disc sander to do this but you can use a block plane instead. Then draw around the template on the already slotted workpieces.

9 Fix both rack ends together with carpet tape and bandsaw them close to the drawn line. Clean the shapes up to the line as you did for the template.

10 In order to remove any grain tearing and get rid of sharp edges, use a block plane to bevel the edges on both faces of the rack ends.

11 Cut all the dividers to length with the veneer grain running from end to end. It doesn't matter if the dividers are over-width. What I did was to sit the components in the slots of one rack end to check they all fitted together correctly, fitting the back and base first. Then round over the front edges on the router table as seen here; I used a small multiprofile cutter.

12 Sand all faces with an orbital sander. Run glue in all the slots and carefully assemble the whole rack on end. Make sure the back and base still meet when the glue is in place. Tug the shelves forward so there is no visible gapping in the slots. Use a handy weight on the top to hold all the components together.

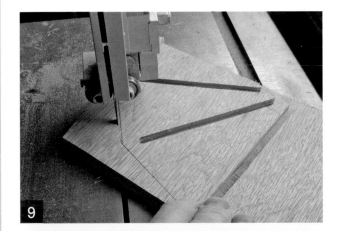

13 Any minor projection underneath one of the rack ends should be sanded off in situ by rubbing on an abrasive sheet so that the rack is not susceptible to rocking.

14 An abrasive 'bat' is a great way to sand edges and still keep them flat. Use it on the bevels as well, so the whole thing is ready to take a finish.

15 Cut out all the drawer components except the base. The drawer front should be a tight or 'plug' fit. The drawer sides and rear can be about 1/16in (2mm) lower on top. The drawer front is rebated using a small tenon cutter so the sides sit in just a fraction; otherwise the drawer will not run. The sides have rebates for the drawer back. Make sure the assembled width is correct at the rear of the drawer. For both this and the next step, make sure you use a push block which is truly square.

16 The base rebates are now complete, and wide enough so that the 1/4in (6mm) base sits in by about 1/32in (1mm) on either side. Add identifying marks to the drawer sides so that you create a perfectly matched opposite pair and avoid any error.

17 The drawer box is glued and pinned using veneer pins, which are punched in and filled over. Check for square and once set, cut, glue and fit the base, weighting it in place until dry.

18 Now for the messy bit. I used spirit dye and wore rubber gloves to keep the dye off my fingers. Apply repeatedly for an even effect. Lay the rags outside to dry, thus avoiding any risk of rapid oxidation, which can cause fire. Light coats of spray lacquer rubbed down between coats, followed by a final waxing, completes the job. I used a ready-made drawer knob, but you can turn your own if you have a lathe. Now let's hope the postman doesn't just bring bills!

MINI CHEST
OF DRAWERS

This little set of drawers is a good exercise in orderly
and accurate parts preparation and basic table-machining
technique. There is more to it than might appear!

This small set of drawers would look good in the bathroom, kitchen, bedroom or lounge, depending on finish and colour. MDF was used for the carcass because it takes paint well. The drawers are made from birch ply, which is easy and pleasant to machine and has a quite subtle grain pattern that was brought out by finishing with clear aerosol lacquer. Chrome drawer knobs lightened the look of the piece.

Cutting list

MDF for carcass
Sides　2 @ 15¾ x 5⅞ x ⅜in (400 x 150 x 9mm)
Top and bottom　2 @ 6¹⁄₁₆ x 5⅜ x ⅜in (154 x 137 x 9mm)
Drawer dividers　4 @ 5¼ x 5⅜ x ⅜in (134 x 137 x 9mm)
Back panel　1 @ 15¼ x 6¹⁄₁₆ x ¼in (388 x 154 x 6mm)
NB: Measure finished carcass openings before making drawers

Birch ply for drawers
Fronts　5 @ 5½ x 2⅝ x ⅜in (140 x 67 x 9mm)
Backs　5 @ 5⅛ x 2⅝ x ⅜in (130 x 67 x 9mm)
Sides　10 @ 5 x 2⅝ x ⅜in (126 x 67 x 9mm)
Bottoms　5 @ 4⅞ x 5⅛ x ⅛in (123 x 130 x 3mm)

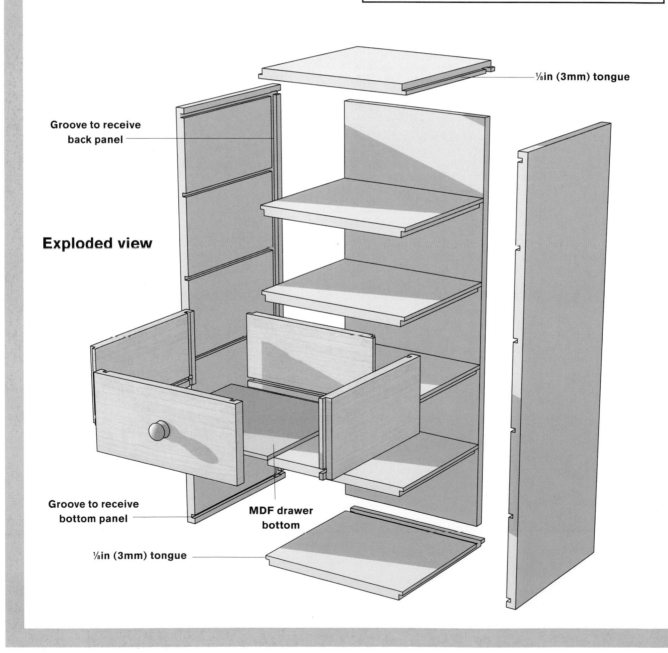

⅛in (3mm) tongue

Groove to receive back panel

Exploded view

Groove to receive bottom panel

MDF drawer bottom

⅛in (3mm) tongue

Plan/section of chest

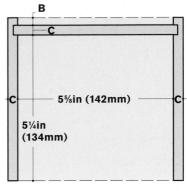

5⅝in (142mm)

5¼in (134mm)

Plan of drawer

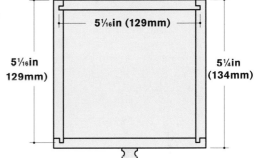

5½in (139mm)

5¹⁄₁₆in (129mm)

5¹⁄₁₆in 129mm)

5¼in (134mm)

Key

A = ⁵⁄₃₂in (4mm)
B = ⁹⁄₃₂in (7mm)
C = ⅜in (9mm)

Cross section

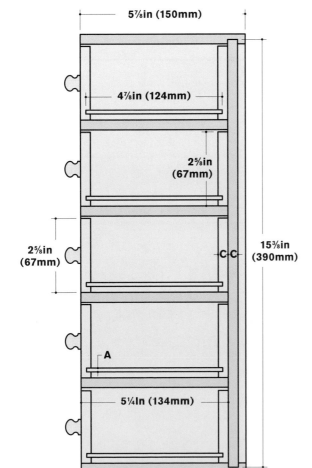

5⅞in (150mm)

4⅞in (124mm)

2⅝in (67mm)

2⅝in (67mm)

15⅜in (390mm)

A

5¼In (134mm)

5⅞in (150mm)

Front elevation/section

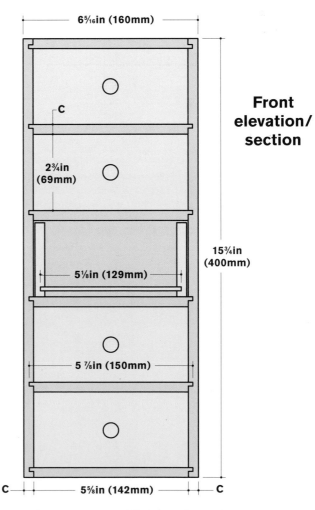

6⁵⁄₁₆in (160mm)

C

2¾in (69mm)

5⅛in (129mm)

15¾in (400mm)

5 ⅞in (150mm)

C   5⅝in (142mm)   C

1 Cut out the carcass parts, excluding the back panel, which will be cut to fit later. Put the two sides together and mark all the drawer dividers across both components, to be sure they match; mark the edges too. The construction will be tongue and groove, so you need to mark the tongue positions too. The tongues will be at the top of each divider, as you view the drawer carcass when it is standing up. The exception is the top one: this must have its tongue on the underside, otherwise the joint will become an unintentional rebate, which is far weaker.

2 Machine all the grooves in the carcass sides, holding the work firmly against the fence and using your edge marks for guidance. Do one half of each side, then turn it round to make the three grooves at the other end. Do not forget that the position of the topmost slot is different, so the fence must be adjusted slightly to suit. I used an ⅛in (3.2mm) straight cutter for this work.

3 All the grooves are now correctly cut. The dividers need to have a rebate machined at each end so they are a good tight fit in the grooves. Note that the four middle dividers are not so deep, because a back panel will be fitted behind them. Make sure you cut all like components at the same time so they match, and have an extra blank or two in case you need to get a better fit. Do not keep testing the joints repeatedly, as the MDF will start to break up and the fit will become looser.

4 Check that the dividers all sit in their grooves nicely and the drawer spacings are correct. Machine a groove along one long edge of the sides and matching grooves in the top and bottom to take a thin ply back panel.

5 The back panel is cut to size and inserted in the grooves at the rear of the carcass, which is now glued and clamped. Check the carcass is square and wipe away any surplus glue.

6 Cut sufficient strips of birch ply for the drawers and check that they fit in the openings. You may need to allocate specific strips to each opening if there are minor size differences. Have some spare material because these drawers use more than you might imagine. Keep each set of drawer components together and mark which position they will fit in.

7 Once again the construction is tongue and groove, with the bottom panels let into a groove all round the inside. The components are quite narrow, and I opted to use a through fence so they would run smoothly over the cutter. You can also help this operation by using a square push block.

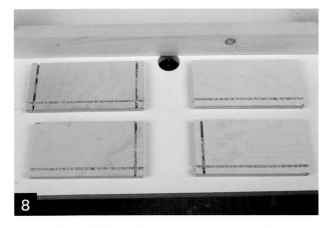

8 Here are the components for one drawer laid out to show the grooves required. The sides and the back panel will now need a rebate to form the tongues.

9 Here the tongue is being formed on a drawer side. The convention for drawers with an integral front panel is that the front panel covers the sides that are jointed into it, whereas the sides fit over the ends of the back panel; this construction is strong and ensures that the drawer sides slide easily inside the carcass.

10 Check the fit of each drawer before gluing them together. If they are tight from side to side, you can trim the back panel a fraction and rerun the rebate cut so the drawer will slide in properly.

11 Cut the drawer bottoms to size and glue and assemble each drawer. Clamp up and, once the glue is dry, check the fit once more; you may need to number the drawers underneath so you know where each one fits best. Break the arrises (edges) with an abrasive 'bat' – a sheet of abrasive spray-mounted to a piece of ply – so there are no sharp or ragged edges to catch yourself on.

12 Now comes the fun of choosing suitable hardware. I don't recommend buying online, as you need to check your choice against an actual drawer. Although the finish is important, size also matters: too small and you cannot grip the knob, too large and it will look clumsy and out of proportion. Try to find a hardware dealer you can visit, and take one drawer along with you. They should be happy for you to go through their stock to make the right choice.

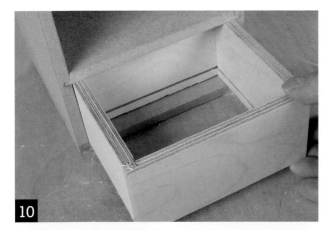

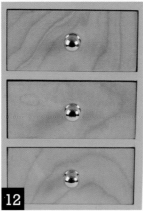

PIGEONHOLE RACK

This simple and versatile design could easily be resized to suit, say, wine bottles or spice jars. It needs to be fixed flat against a wall so nothing can drop down behind, unless you choose to add a back panel of thin ply or MDF.

Making the pigeonhole rack is a repetitive job, requiring a fair number of identical joints which must all be equally accurate. As usual, a simple purpose-built jig makes light of the whole process.

Getting ready

1 Since the router is the key to this project, begin by selecting your cutters. The larger straight cutter is for making the guide bush slots; the smaller one should match the thickness of the timber or board you are using. If you use standard-thickness boards the fit might be a little loose, but some careful glue work and cleaning up should help here. The small roundover cutter will be worked along all the front edges to make the work look and feel better to the touch.

Making the jig

2 The joints used are cross-halving joints and are barefaced, which means the sides are shouldered like a tenon. This means the fit has to be very neat and so, of course, a jig is needed. Rather than make a one-slot jig, I made mine with a whole series of slots, so it is possible to machine the widest components in one go. Note that the jig should allow a cut that goes slightly further than half the width of the wood.

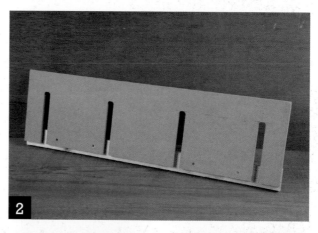

3 Decide on the pigeonhole openings, which will all be one size. Many business letters are in the DL format (which is A4 folded into three), but personal letters and cards are often larger in the shortest dimension, so I sized mine to suit those. Choose your own pigeonhole size to suit the way you want to use the rack. Mark out the slot positions on a piece of MDF or ply which will form the basis of the jig.

4 Prepare your stock, if you are using solid wood, to a thickness that suits the cutter you plan to use. If you are using ply, as I did, make sure you have a cutter that matches its thickness.

5 Before you can mark out the jig slots, you need to work out the difference between the cutter size you are going to use and the guide bush you will need. The slots in the jig will need to be a good match for the diameter of the guide bush.

6 A short router T-square, easily made from offcuts, is an invaluable guide when laying out the jig slots.

7 Mark out the slot positions, leaving an overhang at each end – in this case, 2in (50mm). This is part of the design and makes the outer joints possible. (In this picture we see the spacing being checked for accuracy after the first two slots have been cut.)

8 With the T-square clamped to your jig strip, machine one edge of the first slot. Make sure you put the T-square on the good side, so you always cut into the waste just in case the router moves accidentally off course.

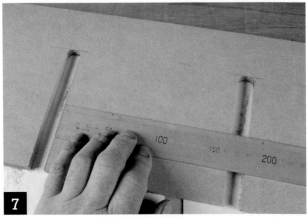

9 Move the T-square across to the other side of the intended slot and make the second cut to arrive at the final width. Put the intended guide bush in place and jiggle it to ensure it is a good fit – not loose, but not too tight.

10 Now glue and screw a small-section batten onto the jig to serve as a fence; this will keep the jig located exactly against the edge of each component.

Making the pigeonholes

11 Machine all your timber or ply to its final width. The end of each cut will be left rounded by the router bit, and when the joints are assembled, the components need to be flush on the edges. That is why the slots in the cross-halving jig need to be long enough to allow you to cut a little more than halfway across each piece.

12 Set up the router and cutter and make a test joint to check the fit. It's better to know at this stage whether the joints will go together properly.

13 In this case the slots aren't quite long enough. Because the discrepancy is small, the simplest solution is to leave the jig as is; before the rack is assembled, the end of each slot can be trimmed slightly with a sharp chisel for a flush fit.

14 Make sure you have overlong boards for all the components you will need. Towards the corners of the rack the boards get quite short; it is best to keep these double length until the slots are cut, then cut them in half afterwards.

15 Trim the ends of the boards at 2in (50mm) beyond the outermost slot, and separate the shorter sections at the outside of the rack.

16 Set up the router table with a small roundover cutter to shape the front edges and the ends of all components.

17 Mark up all components so you know which edges need to be rounded. Bear in mind that when the rack is assembled, half the boards will have their joints forward while the other half will have continuous edges forward. Start by routing the long edges from both faces.

18 Now machine all the ends in the same fashion, supporting the board with both hands.

19 Sand all faces with an orbital sander, and all edges with folded abrasive, working by hand. Make sure the edges are completely smooth, especially if the material is ply.

20 Use a piece of board to protect the edges while tapping the components together.

21 Finally, apply varnish in several coats, flatting between coats to obtain a good finish.

JEWELLERY TREE

This scrollsaw project uses a mahogany-like hardwood for both base and tree; high-quality plywood could be a good alternative, and would reduce any worries about grain direction.

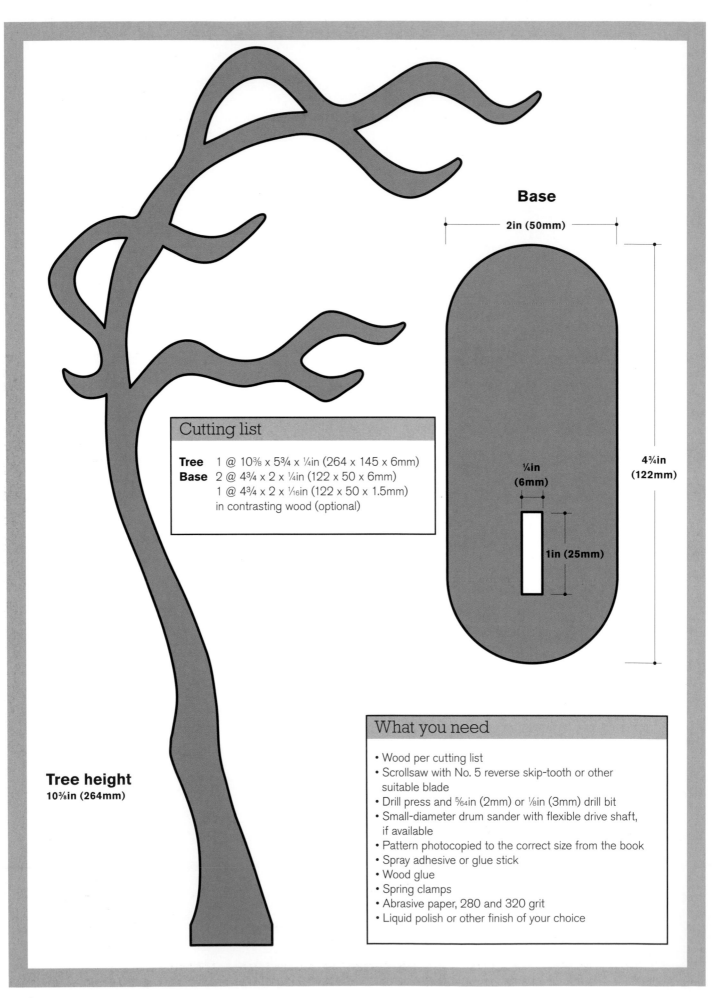

Base

2in (50mm)

4¾in
(122mm)

¼in
(6mm)

1in (25mm)

Cutting list

Tree 1 @ 10⅜ x 5¾ x ¼in (264 x 145 x 6mm)
Base 2 @ 4¾ x 2 x ¼in (122 x 50 x 6mm)
1 @ 4¾ x 2 x ¹⁄₁₆in (122 x 50 x 1.5mm)
in contrasting wood (optional)

Tree height
10⅜in (264mm)

What you need

- Wood per cutting list
- Scrollsaw with No. 5 reverse skip-tooth or other
  suitable blade
- Drill press and ⁵⁄₆₄in (2mm) or ⅛in (3mm) drill bit
- Small-diameter drum sander with flexible drive shaft,
  if available
- Pattern photocopied to the correct size from the book
- Spray adhesive or glue stick
- Wood glue
- Spring clamps
- Abrasive paper, 280 and 320 grit
- Liquid polish or other finish of your choice

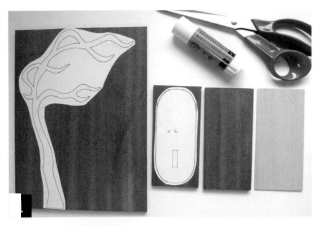

Getting started

1 Begin by choosing your wood and then cutting it to size. Make one copy of each pattern, aligning the long dimension of the base and the stem of the tree with the grain of the wood; attach them with either spray adhesive or a glue stick.

2 Drill the blade starter holes in the base and the tree section. The size of the bit is determined by the size of the inner piece that is to be removed; in this case, 5/64in (2mm) or 1/8in (3mm) would be fine.

Making the base

3 Set up the scrollsaw with a No. 5 reverse skip-tooth blade, thread the blade through the pre-drilled hole in the top layer of the base and reattach in the usual way. Cut into the corner…

4 …and then back the blade out just enough to make the turn to continue along the cutting line.

5 Once the bulk of the waste is removed, return to each corner in turn to finish the cut.

6 Next, leaving the pattern intact, apply wood glue evenly to the underside of this piece and to the remaining 1/4in (6mm) blank.

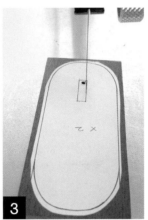

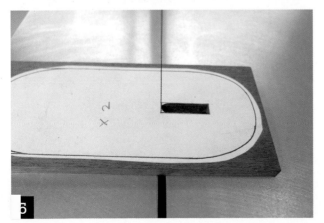

7 Align and laminate the three base pieces together, clamp to secure, and wipe away any excess glue within the hole; then set to one side to dry completely.

8 When the glue is fully cured, cut carefully around the perimeter.

Making the tree

9 As with the base of the project, cut out and remove the inner openings first…

10 …then cut around the outer edges, finally returning to clean out the corners.

Finishing touches

11 Peel off the patterns and round over the edges to give a more finished look. A small-diameter drum sander attached to a flexible drive shaft is ideal for this, if you have one. Follow this with hand-sanding, going through the grades for a really smooth finish, being mindful not to put too much pressure on any sections of the tree that go across the grain.

12 Glue the tree into the base and remove any excess. When dry, apply a finish of your choice; liquid polish will bring out the natural beauty of the wood.

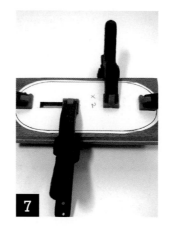
7

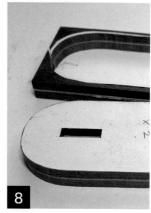
8

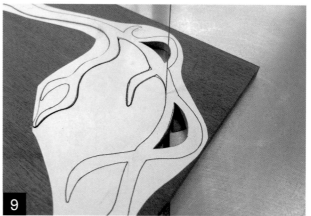
9

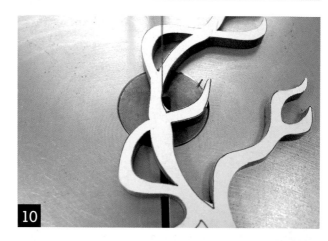
10

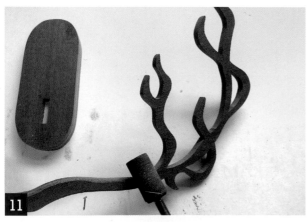
11

12

SMALL SHELVES

These painted shelves may not have a high storage capacity, but they are easy to make and will brighten a gloomy corner. You may even have all the materials you need in your scrap box.

Every workshop gets cluttered up with offcuts over time, and rather than torching all the waste board, why not use it to make something fun like this engagingly asymmetrical set of shelves? It needs a little care to make this project work but it isn't difficult to make.

What you need

- ½in (12mm) MDF for the shelves
- 1¼in (30mm) dowel for the uprights
- Scraps of veneer
- Bandsaw
- Drill press (pillar drill) with sawtooth or Forstner bit; alternatively, hand-held drill and flatbit
- Router and top-bearing-guided template cutter
- Oscillating spindle sander, if available
- Home-made sanding bat
- Double-sided tape
- Bench grippers
- Digital callipers
- Wood glue
- Small oval nails
- Utility knife
- Mirror plates
- Wall plugs and screws
- Paint or other finish of your choice

Front elevation

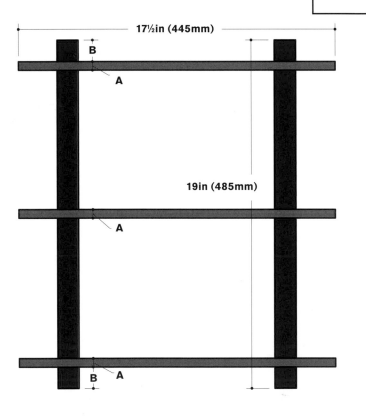

Key

A = ½In (12mm)
B = 1¼in (30mm)
C = Ø 1³⁄₁₆in (30mm)
Ø = overall diameter

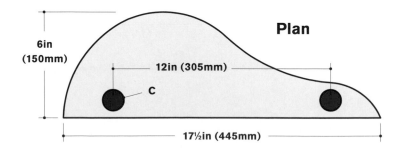

Plan

1 This piece is not meant to be straight and square, so the shape is laid out strictly by hand, creating overlapping pencilled arcs with a twist of the wrist. A large-diameter dowel will be used to hold the shelves together, so I have marked the dowel positions – but I had to change these later when I decided that I wanted to have the middle shelf flipped the other way round.

2 The first shelf is cut on the bandsaw, right on the pencil line, taking great care to create smooth, flowing curves.

3 My favourite 'sanding bat' – a flat piece of wood with sandpaper glued to one side – is used to smooth the outside curves, working repeatedly around the curve until it is even, but also very square across on the edge.

4 The inner curves are harder to keep nice and crisp in profile, but luckily I have an oscillating spindle sander and it creates flowing internal curves quickly.

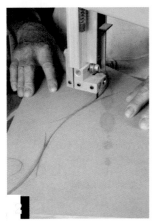

5 The other two shelves are marked out by drawing round the first one onto another piece of board.

6 In order to get exact copies of the first shelf, the other two are routed using a top-bearing-guided template cutter. Double-sided tape is used to fix the three pieces together so that the first one can serve as a template.

7 The whole pack, with the template shelf on top, is placed on 'cookie'-shaped bench grippers so the cutter cannot mark the bench surface beneath.

8 The three identical shelves are now ready for marking and drilling to take the large-diameter dowel. Finding a ready-made dowel that exactly matches a cutter size is a tall order, but a quick check shows that I have one just a fraction oversize, and this is near enough. These digital callipers are easy to zero and give a precise readout that is easy to see and to understand.

9 Having swapped the middle shelf around, I had to re-mark the dowel holes so they were in exactly the same position at each end.

10 You can use a flatbit in a hand-held drill, but a small pillar drill makes a much more accurate job of it and has a small footprint that suits a small workshop. **Warning:** The guard is raised here for clarity; ensure that it is in place before you start drilling.

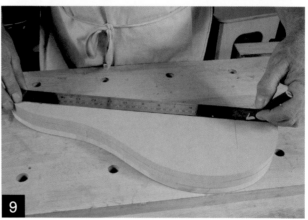

11 The dowels are identically marked and the shelves are slid into position. The dowels are a loose fit, but we will deal with that shortly.

12 Tiny oval nails are used to pin the shelves in their marked positions. Then slips of veneer with glue applied are pushed into the gaps around the dowels. A new knife blade is used to trim off excess veneer and the glue is wiped away. Lay the shelves flat, check for square and leave to set. When dry, paint the shelves in a suitable colour scheme and attach a couple of small mirror plates so they can be fixed to the wall with wallplugs and screws.

PEG RAIL

Originally designed for displaying colourful scarves in an upmarket gallery, these peg rails will look equally at home in your hall, keeping the family's coats and accessories in one place.

These pegs were commissioned by a gallery to display scarves and other accessories. English oak (*Quercus robur*) was the material chosen, and the pegs were relatively large, with a ball end rather than a Shaker-style mushroom end, so the items would be a little more secure. If you think these pegs too large for a domestic situation, it will be a simple matter to scale them down.

When using oak which has been sawn through and through (slabsawn), there is usually a strip of sapwood along one or both edges. The board I used had sapwood along one edge and a few shakes near the other edge, which had been at the centre of the tree; I had to start by removing these.

Cutting list

To make one W-shaped peg rail; extra allowances given on lengths only. Use oak (*Quercus* sp.) or similar.

Peg rail   4 @ 12¼ x 2 x ⅞in (311 x 50 x 22mm)
Pegs   5 @ 7½ x 1 x 1in (190 x 25 x 25mm)

What you need

- Timber per cutting list
- Scrap timber to make halving jig
- Bandsaw with ½in (12mm) skip-tooth blade
- Planer-thicknesser
- Router with straight cutter and self-guiding roundover bit
- Palm sander
- Lathe
- Spindle roughing gouge
- Large skew chisel
- Small parting tool
- Large scraper
- Centre finder, if available
- Flush-cutting saw
- Clear wax polish

Peg rail
Not to scale

31¼in (792mm)

E

A

F

10in (255mm)

12in (305mm)

E

9⅞in (251mm)

Key

A = Ø ½in (12.5mm)
B = ½in (12.5mm)
C = Ø ⅞in (22mm)
D = ⅞in (22mm)
E = 1in (25mm)
F = 2in (50mm)
Ø = overall diameter

6in (152mm)

D

B

E

C

C

Peg
Scale 1:2

The rail

1 Draw a straight line near one edge of the board to mark the extent of the sapwood. Using a bandsaw fitted with a ½in (12mm) skip-tooth blade, saw along the marked line so that all the sapwood is removed.

2 Next, plane the sawn edge to provide a straight surface to bear against the bandsaw fence.

3 Adjust the fence so that the maximum width can be obtained while eliminating any shakes or defects.

4 Use the planer to plane one face of each board flat, and then pass them through the thicknesser a few times to finish with a thickness of about ⅞in (22mm).

5 The W-shape is joined together with halving joints, which after gluing together will be reinforced by the ½in (12.5mm) tenons that are turned on the ends of the pegs. Form the halving joints across the whole width of the board, using a router guided by the jig shown here, or by a straight piece of wood clamped to the surface. Set the straight cutter used in the router so that it takes out exactly half the depth of the wood. It is advisable to try this on a piece of scrap first.

6 Now saw the wood into strips before planing the edges to finish with pieces 2in (50mm) wide.

7 Trim the length of the halvings, allowing a little extra for further trimming after they are glued together. Apply glue to one face of each joint and then hold in position with G-clamps until set.

8 Trim any slight projections at the ends, then sand smooth. Because of the opposing grain direction, a small orbital sander, or palm sander, is useful when sanding flat and level.

9 Using a drill press to ensure the holes are vertical, drill a ½in (12mm) diameter hole at each peg position. To complete the peg rail, work a ¼in (6mm) radius all round the W using a self-guiding roundover bit in a router.

Turning the pegs

10 To turn the pegs you will need blanks which are 1in (25mm) square by about 7½in (190mm) long to allow for mounting between centres and trimming. Prepare the blanks for turning by marking the diagonals at each end; easier still is to use a commercial centre finder, if you have one. If you trim the corners of the blanks at a 45° angle on the bandsaw it will save a little time when turning.

11 Mount the blank between centres and use a spindle roughing gouge to shape it to a cylinder. Then with a large skew chisel plane the cylinder smooth; to avoid a dig-in you should only use the centre third of the blade for this operation.

12 With a small parting tool, narrow the end down to mark the top end of the ball.

13 Use the short end of the skew chisel to form the upper end of the ball. Repeat this operation to complete the ball down to the diameter of the upper part of the peg.

14 With a shallow spindle roughing gouge, followed by the skew chisel, continue shaping the shaft of the peg.

15 Form a sharp edge at the base of the stem, using the long corner of the skew chisel. To avoid a dig-in, just cut with the extreme point angled slightly away from the surface you are forming, then use a parting tool to complete the tenon down to ½in (12mm) diameter.

16 Use the skew to true up the base of the peg so it forms an accurate shoulder for the tenon. Now check to make sure your tenons are a good fit in the holes. If you are using a softwood such as pine (*Pinus* sp.), the diameter can be a little oversize because the wood, being soft, will compress slightly when entering the hole; but when using oak, as I did, you are more likely to split the backing board if you are not careful. Mount the tenon in a chuck and use a large scraper to trim the ends. Sand the pegs to 240 grit, then burnish them with a handful of shavings.

Final assembly

17 To avoid squeeze-out, apply glue to the holes drilled in the rail but not to the tenons, then insert the pegs. When set, trim the ends of the tenons with a flush-cutting saw. After sanding the back, the pegs and board are finished with a coat of clear wax polish.

18 All that remains is to drill and countersink a pair of holes through which the peg rail can be fixed to the wall.

SPOON RACK

This open-fronted display case, made specially for a collection of miniature silverware, has an understated elegance that sets off its contents to perfection and does not overwhelm them.

The 24 spoons worked well as four rows of six; by using a mix of sizes in each row, I could have equal spaces between the shelves and between the individual spoons To hang well, a small hole was needed for the shoulder of each spoon to sit in, about ³⁄₈in (10mm) diameter. The spoon handles would not all go through that hole, so an entry slot would be needed from the front of the shelf into each hole.

Key

A = ⅛in (3mm)
B = ¼in (6mm)
C = ⅜in (10mm)
D = Ø ⅜in (10mm)
E = ¾in (19mm)

F = 1in (25mm)
G = 1½in (38mm)
H = 1¾in (44mm)
J = 2¾in (70mm)
K = 4½in (114mm)
Ø = overall diameter

What you need

- Oak for sides, shelves, top and bottom
- ⅛in (3mm) oak-faced ply for the back panel
- Offcut of ⅛in (3mm) hardboard
- Bandsaw
- Radial-arm saw
- Planer-thicknesser
- Drill press (pillar drill)
- Loose-tenon joiner
- Router and table, ⅛in (3.2mm) quadrant cutter
- Belt sander with side fence
- Random orbital sander
- Palm sander
- Abrasives to 320 grit
- Home-made fuming chamber
- Ammonia .890sg, used with face and hand protection
- Boiled linseed oil
- Grey scouring pad
- Sash clamps
- 'Mouse' plane

Front elevation

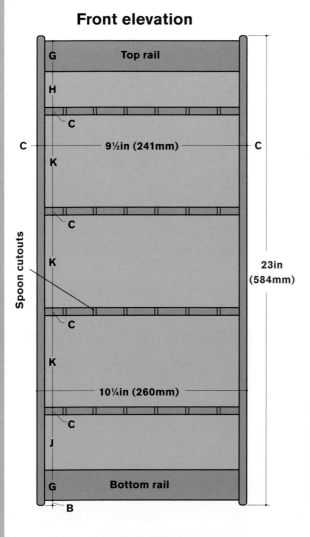

Shelf plan/section

9¾in (248mm)

D G G

Cross section

19¾in (502mm)

Loose tenons

Groove

Back panel

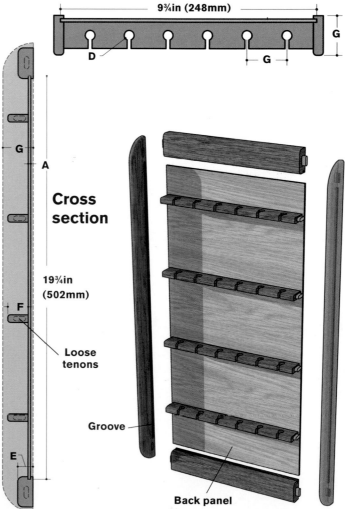

Front elevation labels:
G — Top rail
H
C
C — 9½in (241mm) — C
K
C
K
Spoon cutouts
C
K
10¼in (260mm)
C
J
G — Bottom rail
B
23in (584mm)

The timber

A dark wood with a satin finish to contrast with the shiny silver of the spoons was required. I chose English oak (*Quercus robur*) as it can be fumed to a dark chocolate colour. I selected some nice clean pieces free of sapwood – sapwood contains little tannin and doesn't darken like the heartwood when fumed. The stock had been in my warm, dry workshop for some time so was ready for immediate use. The components were too small to be safely ripped on my radial-arm saw, so the selected pieces were ripped to width and deep-sawn to thickness on the bandsaw, then finally thicknessed on the planer. To ensure even drying of the freshly exposed surfaces, they were stickered and stacked to allow free air circulation.

Construction

I wanted to use loose tenons for speed and efficiency, but my small hand-held joiner was not really designed for timber as thin as this. I had to fit a spacer to the height fence and a false stop to one of the plunge bars to allow for the shallower depth of cut required.

Making the shelves

1 The shelves were cut down to length on the radial-arm saw. The narrow frame fence was fitted to the loose-tenon joiner, centralized, and set to the width of the shelves. A strip of ⅛in (3mm) hardboard was then cut slightly narrower than the shelves and fitted with double-sided tape between the jaws of the narrow frame fence. The height fence was then adjusted, resulting in a central cut in the ends of the shelves.

2 The depth of cut was adjusted and the tenon slots cut in the ends of the shelves. Using an ⅛in (3.2mm) quadrant cutter on the router table, the front edges of the shelves were rounded over.

3 The centres of the holes for the spoon shoulders were marked on one shelf, the other shelves lined up underneath it and the shelves taped together. The holes were then drilled on my pillar drill.

4 The depth of cut was adjusted on the radial-arm saw and, still with the shelves taped together, the entry slots were cut in the centre of each spoon hole.

Top and base

The top and base were cut to the same length as the shelves and similar tenon slots cut in the ends. The front edges were rounded over in the same way as the shelves and a slot was cut in the inner edges to take the back.

The sides

5 The sides were cut to length on the radial-arm saw and the router table set up to cut a stopped housing for the back.

6 The two sides were marked together for the tenon slots to take the shelves, top and base.

7 In order to reduce the plunge depth of the joiner, a piece of plastic water pipe was split and slipped over the plunge bar to act as a stop. This is a simple home-made device that could prove useful elsewhere in future.

8 The narrow frame fence was used to hold the sides while the shelf slots were cut, then removed to cut the top and base slots.

9 The slotted sides match each other exactly.

10 A quadrant curve was marked on the ends of one side…

11 …then the two sides were taped together and the curve was cut on both simultaneously on the bandsaw.

The back

A back panel was cut to size from an offcut of oak-faced ply and sanded to a finish. It would be glued into the housings and pinned to the shelves to give strength and rigidity.

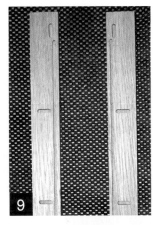

Sanding

12 The curved ends of the sides were sanded and shaped on the inverted belt sander, using the side fence to ensure they were vertical.

13 The remaining components were lightly belt-sanded to remove planer ripples, then random-orbital sanded down to 240 grit.

14 The front edges of the shelves and the sides were finished with a palm sander. A careful inspection was followed by hand-sanding down to 320 grit. Any sanding required after fuming would entail a lot of extra work!

Fuming

15 A fuming chamber was made from an apple box and an empty dust extractor bag. The components were placed inside so that all the surfaces that would be visible on the finished item would be exposed to the gas. Wearing hand and face protection in the open air outside the workshop, I poured a little ammonia .890sg from its container into plastic containers with lids. I carried these into the workshop and slipped them into the bag, removed the lids and quickly sealed the bag. I wanted the oak as dark as possible, so I left it in for the weekend.

12

13

14

15

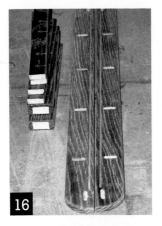

Oiling

16 All the components were oiled before assembly. It is easier to get an even finish when the brush or pad can be 'run off' the ends of the work. Also, if there is any glue ooze on assembly it can be wiped off an oiled surface with a damp cloth, avoiding awkward sanding or scraping of glue that has penetrated bare wood. In order to avoid contamination of the glue joints, the tenon slots were covered with masking tape and thin strips of waste ply were pressed into the stopped housings for the back.

17 Three coats of boiled linseed finishing oil were applied with a cloth pad. After 24 hours each coat was de-nibbed with a grey scouring pad. Wire wool should not be used on oak, as small pieces of the wool get into the grain and are turned black by the tannin in the wood. The final coat was buffed with a soft cloth to a satin sheen.

Assembly

18 Glue was applied sparingly to the relevant slots and loose tenons using a fine brush – the less glue ooze, the better! On a dry run I had established that the clamp pressure closed the spoon entry slots on the shelves rather than pulling up the joints, so I pushed a biscuit into each slot to even out the clamp pressure.

19 Sash clamps were applied and the diagonals checked to ensure the piece was square. It was then laid flat on the bench and left to cure. Once cured, the very little glue ooze that had occurred was removed with my flush-cutting 'mouse' plane and a final very light coat of oil was applied and buffed off.

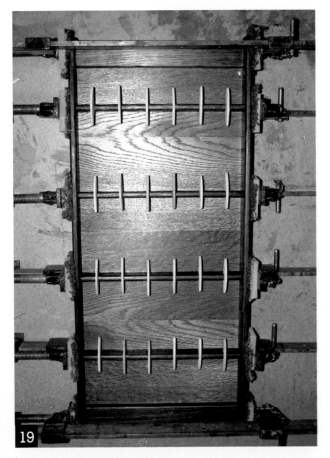

KEY CUPBOARD

This router-based project needs only a small amount of timber. Use whatever wood you have, but if possible select an attractively figured piece for the door panel to contrast with the frame.

Cutting list

Sides	2 @ 11¹³⁄₁₆ x 3⁵⁄₃₂ x ½in	(300 x 80 x 12mm)
Ends	2 @ 7⅞ x 3⁵⁄₃₂ x ½in	(200 x 80 x 12mm)
Back (ply)	1 @ 11³⁄₁₆ x 7¼ x ⁵⁄₃₂in	(284 x 184 x 4mm)
Stiles	2 @ 10⅞ x 1⁹⁄₁₆ x ²⁵⁄₃₂in	(276 x 40 x 20mm)
Rails	2 @ 4²³⁄₃₂ x 1⁹⁄₁₆ x ²⁵⁄₃₂in	(120 x 40 x 20mm)
Door panel	1 @ 7⅞ x 4²¹⁄₃₂ x ⅝in	(200 x 118 x 15mm)
Hook battens	2 @ 7³⁄₃₂ x ⅜ x ¼in	(180 x 10 x 6mm)

What you need

- Timber and plywood per cutting list
- Bandsaw
- Tablesaw or mitre saw
- Planer-thicknesser
- Router table, ⁵⁄₃₂in (4mm) diameter straight cutter, rail and stile cutter set, panel-raising cutter, featherboard, push stick
- Frame clamp
- Bar clamps
- PVA glue
- Abrasive paper
- Flush hinges
- Hand plane if needed
- Doorknob
- Catch
- Oil or lacquer

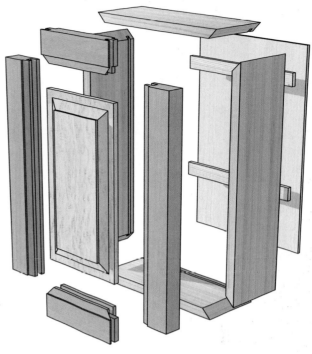

Key
A = ⁵⁄₃₂in (4mm)
B = ¼in (6mm)
C = ½in (12mm)

D = ⅝in (15mm)
E = ¾in (18mm)
F = 1¼in (30mm)
G = 1⁹⁄₁₆in (40mm)

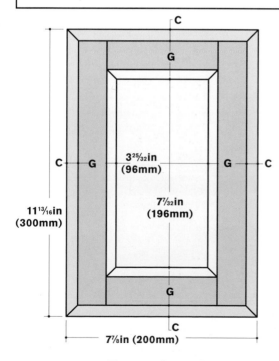

Front elevation

3²⁵⁄₃₂in (96mm)
7⁷⁄₃₂in (196mm)
11¹³⁄₁₆in (300mm)
7⅞in (200mm)

Interior elevation

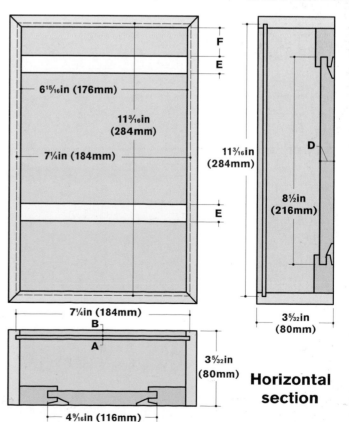

6¹⁵⁄₁₆in (176mm)
11³⁄₁₆in (284mm)
7¼in (184mm)
7¼in (184mm)
4⁹⁄₁₆in (116mm)

Cross section

11³⁄₁₆in (284mm)
8½in (216mm)
3⁵⁄₃₂in (80mm)

3⁵⁄₃₂in (80mm)

Horizontal section

This project needs only a small amount of solid timber and a piece of plywood. I built it as a key cupboard, though obviously it could be used to store other things, too. Its construction involves a fair amount of routing, and to make the panelled door you will need a dedicated cutter set; however, it is all pretty straightforward. The choice of timber is up to you.

Timber preparation

1 You will need some suitable offcuts for this project – chances are you can find something suitable in your scrap box.

2 When cutting up small offcuts, a bandsaw is useful as its thin blade wastes less timber than a tablesaw, leaving more for you to work with.

3 You can now plane and thickness your timber to suit. This piece of cherry (*Prunus* sp.) will become the door frame.

Making the cupboard

4 The cupboard frame is simply made from four boards joined with mitres. Set your tablesaw or mitre saw to 45° and cut to length.

5 The completed sides should look like this.

6 The cupboard back is a piece of ply that is held in a groove cut into the sides. My ply was ⁵⁄₃₂in (4mm) thick, so I fitted the router table with a ⁵⁄₃₂in (4mm) diameter straight cutter.

7 Set the fence about ¼in (6mm) back and set the cutter depth to ⁵⁄₃₂in (4mm). Carefully rout the groove on the inside face of each of the sides. You can now cut your piece of ply to fit.

8 The cupboard can now be assembled. Apply a little glue to each of the joints; you can also run some glue into the groove for the back before fitting the parts together.

9 Support the assembly with a frame clamp and ensure that everything is square by measuring the diagonals to confirm that they match.

Making the door

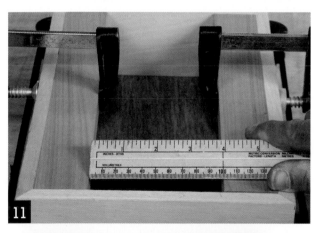

10 Use the assembled cupboard to mark off the length of the door stiles.

11 Cut the stiles to length; they should be a tight fit at this stage. Clamp them in position and measure the gap between them to gauge the length of the rails. Remember that you will need to allow extra length for the joints. A combination rail and stile moulding cutter is ideal for this job. It cuts a joint ⅜in (9.5mm) deep, so you can round this up to ²⁵⁄₃₂in (10mm) and add twice this amount to the length of your rails.

12 Install your cutter in the router table and set it according to the manufacturer's instructions. Normally you cut the joints on the ends of the rails first.

13 In this case the rails are very short, so set up a mitre guide with a sacrificial support board at the rear and then clamp a stop block to it to hold the rail up against the cutter. Now cut the joints on both ends of the rails.

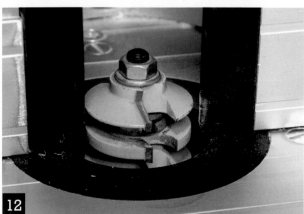

14 The cutter must be reset to cut the grooves in the door frame. Use the rail joint to line up the cutter, then make a test cut using a piece of scrap to make sure that the settings are correct.

15 Again, the short rails need to be treated carefully. Fit a featherboard to the router table so that the workpiece is held tightly against the fence, and also cut a length of scrap to use as a push stick.

16 Fix the relevant cutter guards, start the router and, using the push stick, guide the two short rails past the cutter. Repeat with the stiles.

17 The door frame is now complete.

18 Try to find an interesting piece for the panel. This is bird's-eye maple (*Acer saccharum*). You now need to cut it to the correct dimensions to fit the door frame.

19 Use a panel-raising cutter to mould the edge of the panel so that it fits the groove in the door frame. Some of these cutters have a bearing to guide the workpiece. This one does not, which can cause problems, especially with small panels.

20 Clamp a false fence onto the main fence and raise the cutter to bite into it.

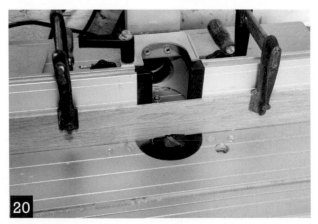

21 When moulding panels, you must take a number of shallow passes until you reach the desired thickness. Test the fit in one of the stiles after each pass until you get a perfect fit.

22 To assemble, apply glue to the joints on the ends of the rails. Be careful not to get any glue on the panel or in its groove. Clamp it up and leave to dry. Because the back of the cupboard is rather thin, fit a pair of battens across it to hold the key hooks. Cut them to length, glue in position and then screw the hooks in.

Hanging the door

23 Mark the positions of the hinges on the door. Line them up with the edge of the frame moulding.

24 Mark the hole positions on the edge of the door. Use flush hinges as they don't need to be recessed into the door or frame.

25 Drill pilot holes and fit the hinges with one screw each.

26 Place the door in the cupboard frame and mark the hinge positions. Adjust the fit of the door with a plane if necessary.

27 Screw the hinges in position, again with one screw each, and check the fit. Make any adjustments and finally insert all the screws.

28 Fit some kind of catch to hold the door shut, and turn or buy a suitable handle. The cupboard now just needs some oil or lacquer and it is ready for use.

SCROLLSAW KEY HOLDER

You'll never lose your keys again if you have a proper place to keep them. This scrollsaw key holder project could make a great house-warming gift, especially if you can modify the design to resemble the recipient's new home.

Although simple, this project does require a fair amount of accuracy, especially when cutting out the windows. There are quite a few parallel lines that will stand out like sore thumbs if they're wobbly instead of perfectly straight!

What you need

- 2 pieces of plywood, 7 x 4½ x ¼in (180 x 115 x 6mm)
- 5 small Shaker-style pegs, or pegs/hooks of your choice
- Scrollsaw with No. 2 and No. 5 reverse skip-tooth blades
- Photocopy of the template, enlarged to fit your material
- Pillar drill with ¹⁄₁₆, ³⁄₁₆, ¼in (1.5, 5, 6mm) bits (and a bit to suit the size of your pegs/hooks, if different)
- Masking tape
- Glue stick or spray adhesive
- Paint (e.g. acrylic) or wood stain
- Wood glue
- G-clamps and/or spring clamps
- Sandpaper, 180, 240, 320 grit
- Hanger of your choice
- Finish of your choice

Template
Photocopy to required size

Getting started

1 First copy the template to the required dimensions and then cut the two wood blanks to size. Sand the top of one blank and the underside of the other, then place masking tape all across the blank that is to be the top one.

2 Attach the template to the top blank, over the masking tape, using spray-mount or glue stick.

3 Use your smallest bit in the pillar drill to drill all the blade pilot holes, then use a ¼in (6mm) bit for inside the letter 'e'.

4 We used a ³⁄₁₆in (5mm) bit to drill the five holes for the Shaker pegs. Use a bit that suits whichever size of peg or hook you plan to use.

Cutting out

5 Set the scrollsaw up with a No. 2 reverse-tooth blade, insert the blade through the first pilot hole and begin by cutting into the first corner.

6 Back the blade up a little to make the turn, then continue along the cutting line to the next corner.

7 Continue in this way until you are back where you started, removing the bulk of the waste.

8 Return to clean out the corners. Try to resist pushing sideways on the blade to pick up the cutting line, as this could result in a distorted line; as all the windows have straight parallel lines, any wobbliness will be quite noticeable.

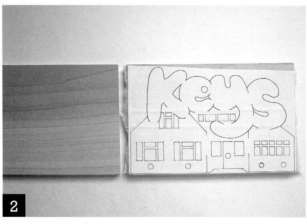

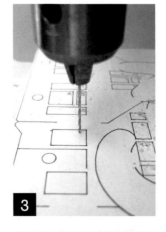

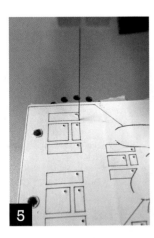

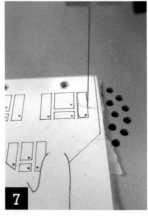

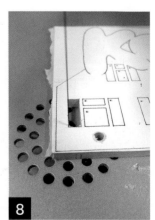

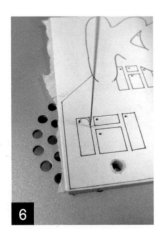

9 Where a window adjoins another part of the template, like the bottom of the letter 'y', just continue to cut along the line…

10 …and then release the blade in the usual way at the end of the cutting line.

11 Sometimes you may need to cut a continuous curve going in both directions from a window. First cut into one side of the curve, then back the blade into the window area again and turn the whole piece around so you can back the blade up into the cut line…

12 …which makes it easier to finish the curve.

13 Use a similar method for the inside cut within the letter 's': start by cutting out and around from the pilot hole to one side of the curve, then back the blade up into the pilot hole again, turn the whole piece around so you can back the blade into the cutting line, and then carry the cut through for a continuous smooth curve.

14 Once all the inner cuts have been made, cut up into the lines that define the house and outline the door. Do not cut around the outer edge at this time, or remove the template.

15 Turn the whole piece over and sand off any burr from all the inner cuts and drilled holes.

Assembly

16 Place the top piece right side up onto the bottom blank and lightly mark the positions of the windows and other openings.

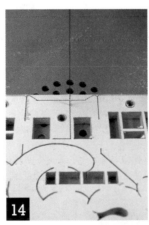

17 Mix a coloured paint or wood stain of your choosing, and paint those areas of the lower piece that will be visible through the openings. Leave to dry.

18 Apply an even coat of glue to the underside of the top. Don't go too close to the windows, or glue may seep out.

19 Place the top piece in position on the bottom blank, clamp to secure – as they say, you can never have too many clamps! – and again leave to dry.

20 Change to a No. 5 reverse skip-tooth blade and cut all around the outer edge of the template.

21 As with the inner cuts, return to the tighter corners to remove the waste.

22 Peel off the template and masking tape and round over all the edges using first 240- then 320-grit sandpaper. Take the time to sand each of the windows, as this will give the key holder a more professional look and feel.

23 Attach the Shaker-style pegs by applying a dab of glue into each of the five holes and then pushing the pegs firmly into place.

24 Apply your finish of choice to the whole piece, including the reverse side; whatever you apply to the surface should also be applied to the back, to help prevent the wood distorting. All that remains now is to attach a hanger to the back – either a picture hanger of some kind or, for greater security, a mirror plate – and you need never mislay your keys again.

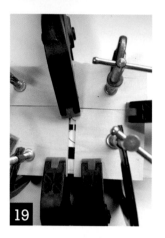

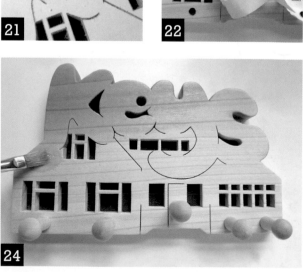

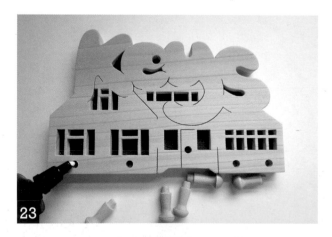

WINDOW BOX

This simple and versatile design can be used indoors or out, either as a planter or as a holder for potted plants. The dimensions given are for a small version; adjust them to suit your own requirements.

The design is not entirely straightforward, because both sides and ends have curved tops and are jointed at a 15° angle. All the components may be cut by hand, but cutting the angles accurately is a lot easier with a tablesaw or mitre saw.

What you need

- Softwood plank, 80½ x 6in (2040 x 150mm), 1in (25mm) nominal thickness, set out as shown opposite
- Mitre saw
- Block plane
- Bandsaw or jigsaw
- Tablesaw, mitre saw or handsaw
- Drill/driver and bits
- Bench-mounted disc sander
- Waterproof glue
- Pin hammer and panel pins, or screwdriver and screws
- Wood preservative
- Thick plastic liner, if the box is to be filled with compost

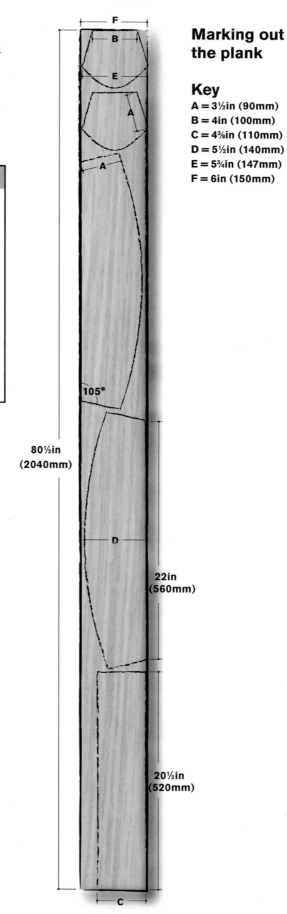

Marking out the plank

Key
A = 3½in (90mm)
B = 4in (100mm)
C = 4⅜in (110mm)
D = 5½in (140mm)
E = 5¾in (147mm)
F = 6in (150mm)

80½in (2040mm)

105°

22in (560mm)

20½in (520mm)

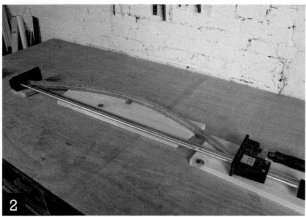

1 Start by marking out the plank. A sanding disc was used here as a template to draw the curve on the ends.

2 To mark the curve on the sides, a long metal rule was compressed in a bar clamp to make it bend. A piece of thin ply could also be used in a similar manner.

3 Cut out the curves using a bandsaw or a jigsaw. Note the relief cuts that have been made in the waste area to reduce the side pressure on the blade.

4 Crosscut the sides to length.

5 The curved sides can also be cut with the bandsaw.

6 Clamp the two sides together in a vice and, using a block plane, clean up the edges so that they match. You could use a sander instead.

7 Tape the ends together and clean up the curves with the block plane or disc sander.

8 Once all the parts are smooth, they can be glued and pinned together. You may prefer to use screws in place of pins, particularly if you are making a large box. Because of the angle, it can be a bit tricky to fit the first joint together, so clamp the end in a vice before attaching the side.

9 Finally, make the base. The edges of this also need to be angled at 15° to match the sides, so use a tablesaw and tilt the blade to suit. It is difficult to measure the exact size of the base, so make it on the large side and then trim it down to fit.

10 Crosscut the ends.

11 Attach the base with glue and pins, and then drill some drainage holes through it. Finally, turn the box upside down and pin a pair of thin battens across the ends to raise it off the ground; this will provide drainage and also help to stop the box from rotting.

12 The box is now complete, but obviously needs a good coating of wood preservative before use. If you want to fill it with earth (rather than keeping the plants in individual pots), line it with thick polythene for protection.

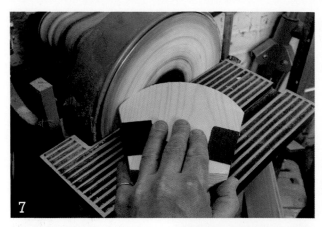

7

8

9

10

11

12

RUSTIC STOOLS

The simple five-plank stool has an enormous range of uses: it is a step to reach a high shelf, a handy seat for all manner of tasks, and an immensely versatile toy for imaginative children.

The five-plank stool is one of the oldest and simplest of furniture designs. Known in the northeast of England as a 'cracket', it was traditionally made by miners from any wood they could find lying around. To withstand the rigours of everyday use, it needs well-fitting, robust joints. There are two stools in this project: one in painted pine (*Pinus* sp.), and a slightly more decorative one in oak (*Quercus robur*).

What you need

- Oak and pine offcuts
- Planer-thicknesser with dust extraction
- Ear defenders
- Bandsaw
- Tablesaw, mitre saw or handsaw
- Jigsaw or fretsaw (or bandsaw with narrow blade)
- Pillar drill with Forstner bit and hold-downs (or brace if preferred)
- Hand-held drill and small bit to make pilot holes for nails
- Bench plane if desired
- Mitre plane and shooting board
- Sliding bevel and protractor (if your mitre saw does not have a laser guide)
- Marking knife
- Nails, hammer and punch
- 2-part epoxy filler (or putty)
- Primer, undercoat and topcoat (for the pine stool)
- Garnet French polish (for the oak stool)

Key

A = ¾in (20mm)
B = ¹¹⁄₁₆in (18mm)
C = 1in (25mm)
D = 1³⁄₁₆in (30mm)

E = 2in (50mm)
F = 2³⁄₁₆in (55mm)
G = 2⅜in (60mm)
Ø = overall diameter

7⅞in (200mm)

A

G

6¹¹⁄₁₆in (170mm)

4⅜in (110mm)

G   3⅛in (80mm)   G

End elevation

13in (330mm)

D

E   A   **Oak stool**   C

Front elevation

9⅛in (230mm)

B

2⁷⁄₁₆in (62mm)

B

7½in (190mm)

Ø ⅝in (15mm)

5½in (140mm)

10⅝in (270mm)

F   4¾in (120mm)   F

14½in (370mm)

G   2⁷⁄₁₆in (62mm)   75°

B   C

Pine stool

1 In keeping with tradition, both stools were made from recycled wood or material left over from other projects. Some of the boards were cupped, but as you can see from the lines drawn on the end of one board, there was still enough to get $^{11}/_{16}$in (18mm)-thick boards from them.

2 The boards were first planed flat with the cupped surface facing down onto the planer bed. Note the use of a push stick to keep fingers away from cutting edges, and the guard set to cover the full width of the cutter block.

3 Here the boards have been faced and edged and are ready for the thicknesser. It's a good idea to wear ear defenders when using a planer or planer-thicknesser.

4 Each piece of wood is run through the thicknesser in turn, starting with the thickest and gradually raising the bed until all the boards are the same thickness. Dust extraction is essential or the machine – and your workshop – will rapidly clog up with shavings.

5 Here are the planed, square-edged boards ready for use. These oak boards were glued together to provide wider boards, clamped up and set aside to dry while work continued on the painted pine stool.

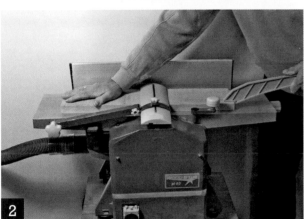

6 The 12in (300mm)-wide pine board was ripped down to create two boards, the wider one to make the top and legs, and the narrower to make the side pieces.

7 Stools like this would have originally been made with hand tools and could still be easily made without machinery. I edge-jointed the pine board with my No. 6 hand plane as a token gesture, but both stools were made using power tools wherever possible.

8 Once the top had been roughly cut to length – you can do this by hand or using a tablesaw or mitre saw – it was trued up using a shooting board and a mitre plane.

9 The centre of the seat piece was then marked for the finger hole…

10 …which was drilled out using a Forstner bit in the pillar drill. Hold-downs kept the board firmly in place for safety and accuracy. The hole could easily be drilled using a hand brace and bit if you feel the need to uphold the handmaking tradition.

11 The sides were cut to length and shape using the mitre saw. No need to mark the angles, just mark the length, set the angle of the saw and align the cut using the laser guide. If your saw does not have a laser, or you are cutting the piece by hand, then you will need to mark out the angle using a sliding bevel or a protractor.

12 The mitre saw was also used to cut the bevel on the leg pieces. This is not critical within sensible margins, but about 15° works well and makes for a sturdy stool. You could do this on the tablesaw, or by hand.

13 The centre of the end pieces and the V for the legs were marked, following the dimensions in the drawing. Again, the exact angles and dimensions are not critical here but those given look balanced and make the stool very stable.

14 The hole for the apex of the triangle was drilled and the legs then cut out. I used the mitre gauge in the bandsaw to help keep the cut aligned.

15 The rebates on the legs were marked where they would fit against the side pieces of the stool. This is best done by working directly from the side pieces for accuracy. I used a pencil to mark them out, but a fine cut from a marking knife would be even more accurate.

16 The long-grain cuts were then made using the bandsaw. I set a stop on the fence to prevent it from overcutting.

17 The angled cross-grain cuts could also be done on the bandsaw by setting the table angle, but with only four small cuts to make it was quicker to do them by hand with a tenon saw.

18 The painted pine stool was constructed in the traditional way using glue and nails. To avoid the nails wandering off course and to centre them, I pre-drilled the nail holes.

19 The sides were glued and nailed first. The nail heads were hammered close to the surface and then a pin punch was used to knock them below the surface; they can be filled later.

20 Once the sides were in place, I located the legs and marked the positions for the nail holes in the side pieces. I used a sliding bevel to mark out the positions of the legs to make sure the holes were centred.

21 Extending the marked lines across the top helped position the nail holes…

22 …which were then drilled, using a sliding bevel to help align the drill.

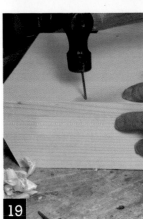

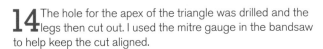

23 The legs were then glued and nailed into position. Mounting the legs in the vice will help to ensure the nails go in straight and true.

24 Once the glue had set, any excess was cleaned away with a sharp knife, the nail holes were filled – traditionally putty would have been used, but I used a modern two-part epoxy filler – and the whole piece was sanded ready for painting.

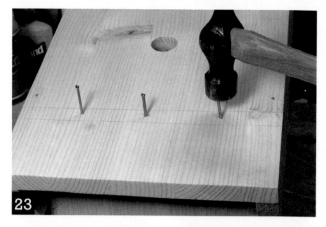

25 The oak stool differs in that the sides and legs have decorative scrolled shapes cut into them. I marked these out by drawing around tins and other round containers, but if you have a set of French curves this will make the job easier. The shapes can then be cut out using a jigsaw, a fretsaw or a bandsaw with a fine blade.

26 The sides and legs were biscuit-joined to the top of the oak stool; the legs are square to the top rather than angled as in the painted pine version.

27 Rather than nailing the sides to the legs of the oak stool, for greater strength and better appearance I used screws. I drilled, countersank and recessed the sides for a wooden plug to cover the screw head.

28 You could make matching plugs with a plug cutter, but I opted for a strong contrast, with plugs made from a dowel turned from a piece of bog oak.

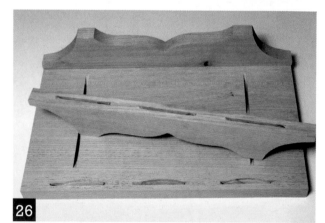

The painted stool was finished with a primer, undercoat and a satin finishing coat, while the oak one was given a few coats of garnet French polish. If your stool is likely to be used – and abused – as a toy or a child's seat, then make absolutely sure you use a toy-safe finish.

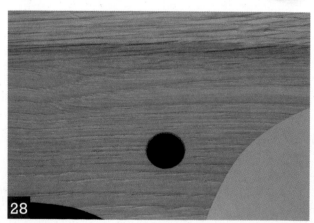

KITCHEN BENCH

There are no complicated joints in this traditional design, which relies on glue and dowels for strength. This type of build is possible because of the effectiveness of modern glues.

Cutting list

Top	1 @ 48 x 11 x ¾in (1220 x 280 x 20mm)
Aprons	2 @ 48 x 3½ x ¾in (1220 x 90 x 20mm)
Legs	2 @ 17 x 11 x ¾in (430 x 280 x 20mm)

What you need

- Pine, per cutting list
- Bandsaw
- Hand-held circular saw with fence
- Random orbital sander
- Drill and 1½in (40mm) bit
- Router and bearing-guided bevel cutter
- Handsaw
- Japanese pullsaw
- Flush-cutting Japanese saw
- Block plane
- Jack plane
- Smoothing plane
- Chisel
- French curve (optional)
- Engineer's square
- Clamps
- 80-grit abrasive glued to wood backing
- Abrasives to 240 grit
- Acrylic satin varnish

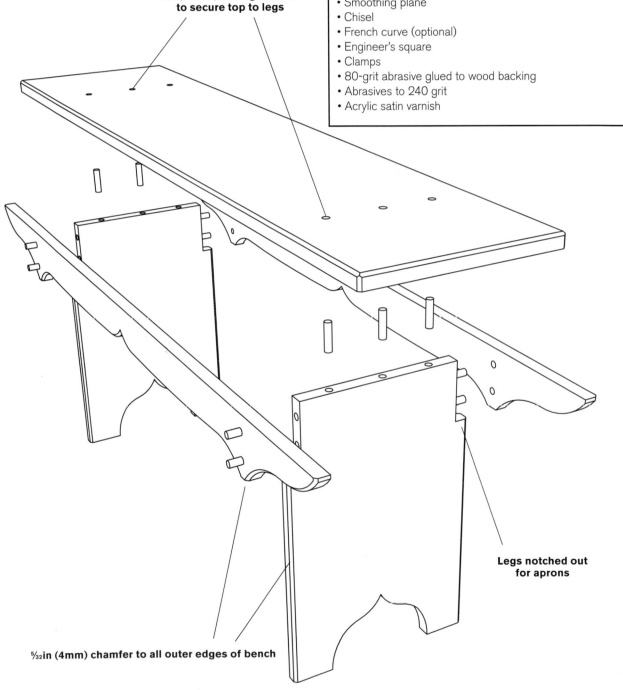

⅜in (10mm) through dowels to secure top to legs

Legs notched out for aprons

⁵⁄₃₂in (4mm) chamfer to all outer edges of bench

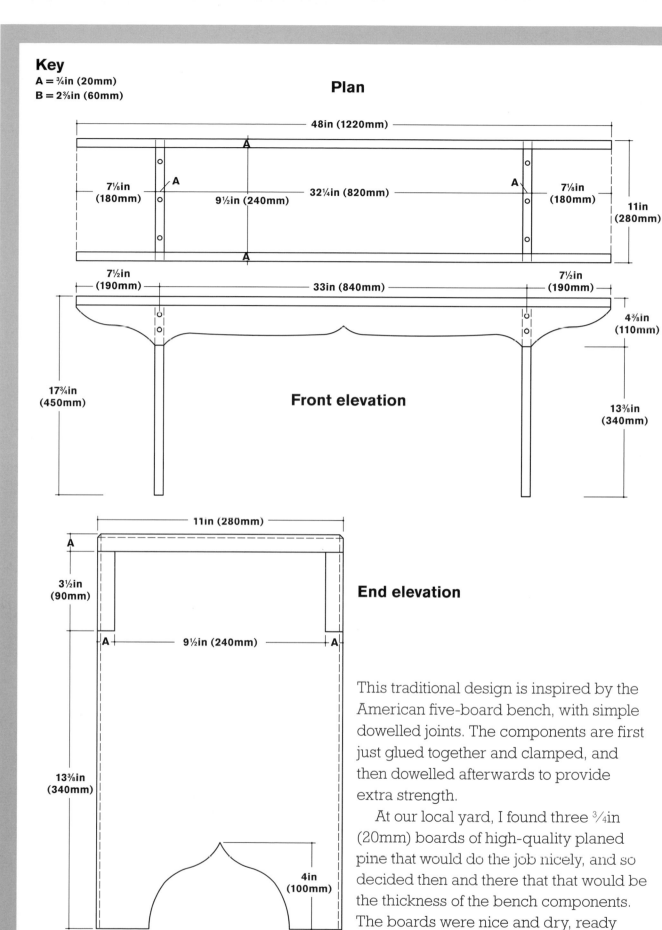

Key

A = ¾in (20mm)
B = 2⅜in (60mm)

Plan

48in (1220mm)

7⅛in (180mm)

9½in (240mm)

32¼in (820mm)

7⅛in (180mm)

11in (280mm)

Front elevation

7½in (190mm)

33in (840mm)

7½in (190mm)

4⅜in (110mm)

17¾in (450mm)

13⅜in (340mm)

End elevation

11in (280mm)

3½in (90mm)

9½in (240mm)

13⅜in (340mm)

4in (100mm)

B

6¼in (160mm)

B

This traditional design is inspired by the American five-board bench, with simple dowelled joints. The components are first just glued together and clamped, and then dowelled afterwards to provide extra strength.

At our local yard, I found three ¾in (20mm) boards of high-quality planed pine that would do the job nicely, and so decided then and there that that would be the thickness of the bench components. The boards were nice and dry, ready for the build.

Part elevation of apron

Part elevation of leg

Key
A = ⁵⁄₃₂in (4mm)
B = ³⁄₈in (10mm)
C = ³⁄₄in (20mm)

3½in
(90mm)

C

A

B

C

A

Overlap dashed lines to give full half profile

Overlap dashed lines to give full half profile

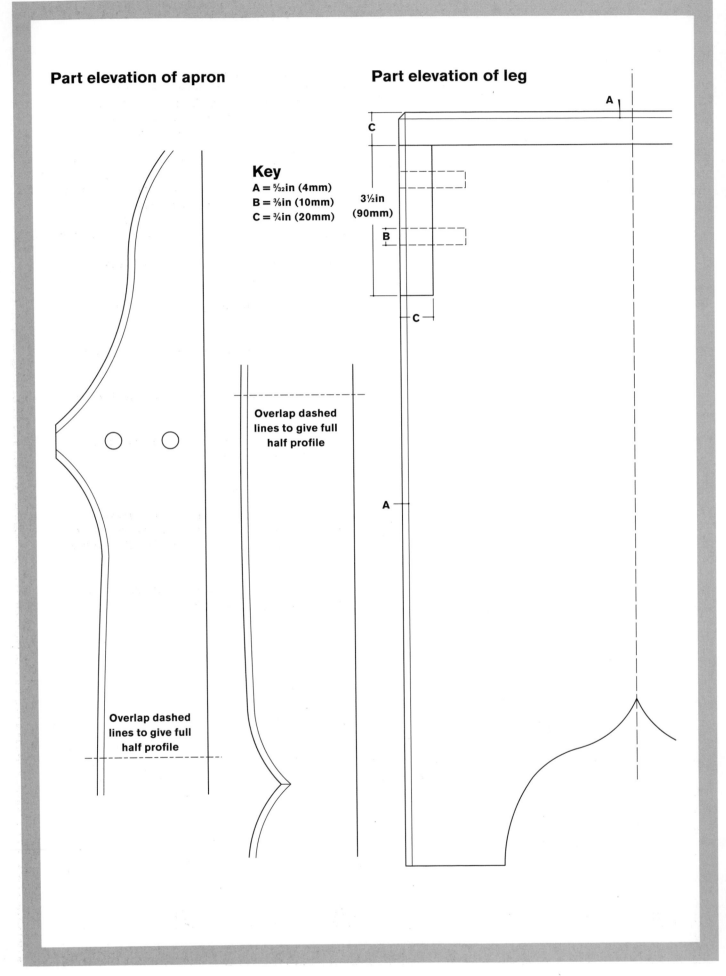

Design

1 With the boards purchased, I set about drawing a pleasing design. A pair of ogee curves that meet at a point in the middle of the timber components was my design motif, and I replicated this design both on the legs and the apron boards, both of which are dowelled to the bench top.

2 I checked for timber defects (such as this resin pocket), and marked up the boards so as to avoid these. One of the boards had a patch of darker heartwood along the middle of it. I decided this board would be perfect for the aprons if cut down the middle, so that the gradient of dark to light timber would become a part of the design of both sides of the bench.

3 I marked square ends on the boards, and measured all the components.

4 For crosscutting boards, I enjoy using a handsaw.

5 I planed off the end grain for a perfectly square and smooth finish.

6 Then I ripped the components outside with a hand-held circular saw…

7 …and squared up and smoothed all the long-grain components with my jack plane.

Shaping the legs

8 You can buy a set of French curves for drawing up designs like this, but I don't mind having a go freehand. First, I experimented with a piece of MDF exactly the same size as the bench legs.

9 When happy with the drawing, I bandsawed this curve out. Note that I only cut half the template.

10 To ensure perfect symmetry, I used the half template to draw one side of the leg cutout…

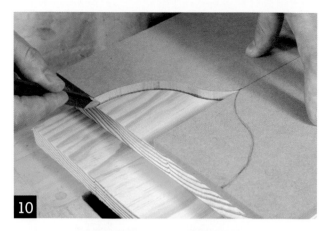

11 …then turned the template over to draw the other half.

12 When bandsawing the legs, I first made plenty of relieving cuts just a fraction inside the outline. If your bandsaw is a small chap like mine, you may have to mark the curves on both sides of the component, then cut one side before turning the component over to cut the other.

13 With the legs cut, I placed them upside down on the bench top to get an idea of proportion, to decide where the legs would be positioned along the bench top and sides.

14 When happy, I marked the positions of the side aprons onto the legs. Direct marking-up like this is always my preferred method, as it cuts out measuring errors, and I drew the design onto one of the apron pieces directly.

15 I cut the housings in the legs, which the aprons fit into, with my trusty Japanese saw.

16 I then pared the housings with a chisel to a perfect finish and fit.

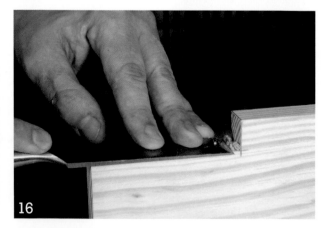

Making the aprons

17 On these pieces I replicated the motif of the double ogee meeting at a point. I drew them freehand again, but you might like to use French curves, or bend and clamp a steel rule in place to draw around.

18 I used the same technique as for the legs, in that I drew up the whole shape, but only cut out half – this half being used as a template to draw out the full design of the other apron piece, which in turn was used to draw the final half of the first piece.

19 I cut out this shape on the bandsaw. Again, you may need to have the design on both sides of the boards, so you can turn the board over to cut out both ends, if your bandsaw table is small.

20 Once all the shapes were cut out, I gave all the component faces a thorough sanding; it's easier to do this now than when everything is glued up.

Assembly

21 Now that everything was cut out and sanded, I then glued and clamped the aprons to the bench underside. I used the legs as spacers to keep the aprons in the correct position while clamping. To help glue-up, you could use a line of biscuits along the underside of the top and the edges of the aprons; this would add extra strength to the construction, too.

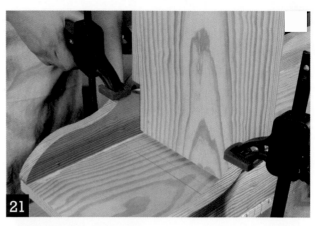

22 Once the glue had gone off, I removed the clamps and started cleaning up the profile of the apron boards. The flats for the leg housings were a touch on the wide side after bandsawing, so I used a sharp chisel to trim these to size.

23 A flat piece of ply with 80-grit abrasive glued around it was then used both to smooth off the shape of the curves and to get rid of the marks left by the bandsaw. You could use a spokeshave and cabinet scraper for this.

24 For the concave shapes, I used the same trick but with the abrasive glued around a dowel instead. You could use a belt sander or any other powered device, but I find it is too easy to round over edges with power tools, so I prefer the slow way, by hand.

25 The faces of the apron boards and the edges of the top were then planed flat and true.

26 After dry-fitting to make any final adjustments to the housings, and ensuring all joint faces were fully in contact, I glued the legs in place, making sure that they were in the correct position along the sides, and square to the bench top. I then clamped the legs in place, all the while checking they didn't move during clamping.

Dowels

27 Once the glue had gone off, it was time to drill the holes for the dowels. I marked the centre line of the legs across the sides and top of the bench, and then marked the dowel hole positions. I used ⅜in (10mm) dowels here. You can make your own dowels or buy ready-prepared ones, whichever you prefer.

28 I would be sinking the dowels to a depth of 1½in (40mm), so I marked this depth on the bit with tape, lined up the drill with an engineer's square and then drilled the holes. Be careful and only use very sharp drill bits, or else you can get breakout on the surface of the timber. An alternative method would be to use a router and drilling bit. Another option is to clamp sacrificial scrap to the bench and drill through that to prevent any breakout.

29 I then applied glue to the holes and dowels, and tapped them home. Make sure your holes are clear of chippings, as you don't want any voids under the dowels, nor do you want to risk splitting the timber.

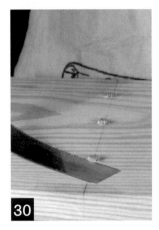

30 Once the glue had dried, I cut off the dowel ends with a flush-cutting saw – I love my Japanese tools!

31 I could now rout a ⁵⁄₃₂in (4mm) 45° bevel on all the outside edges, using a small router and bearing-guided bevel cutter. Great care had to be taken when doing the edges of the legs; you may want to provide additional support for your router base here.

Finishing

32 There were a few small shakes and other small defects in the timber, so I used a colour-matched filler prior to sanding and finishing.

33 I sanded the whole thing down to 240 grit ready to apply three coats of water-based acrylic satin varnish, de-nibbing between coats. This varnish goes on easily, dries quickly and produces a lovely lustre, which is perfect for showing off pine to its best.

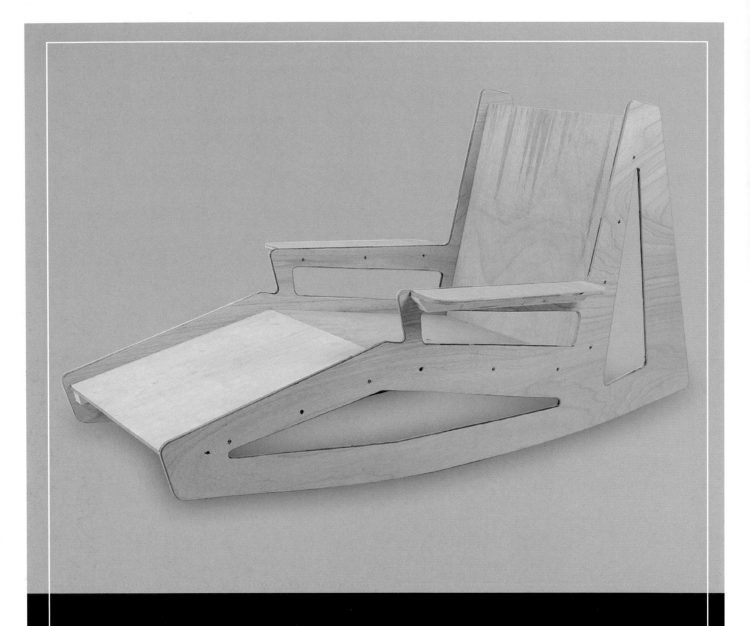

RECLINER

Designing and building seating furniture is tricky, and a recliner that rocks gently is a particularly tall order because the balance has to be just right. Here's a design that really rocks!

This full-length rocking recliner is built entirely from sheet ply. It is a prototype, possibly never to be repeated and certainly with its share of perils and pitfalls. There were various obstacles to overcome, such as how to make it comfortable, suitable for different-sized users and sufficiently pleasant to look at – and, most critical, finding the correct centre of balance. I've made the assumption that at a suitable back angle most of the user's body weight would be towards the rear of the recliner.

What you need

- ⅝in (15mm) plywood for all the flat components
- 1¼in (32mm) square PAR softwood to reinforce the edge joints
- Hardboard or similar for the template
- Jigsaw with straight and scroll-cutting blades
- Mini circular saw with guide rail
- Laminate trimmer with ⅛in (3.2mm) roundover cutter
- Disc sander
- Hand-held drill with combined drill and countersink bit
- Handsaw
- Japanese pullsaw
- Block plane
- Fine-cut rasp
- Sanding 'bat' and 80-mesh abrasive
- Clamps

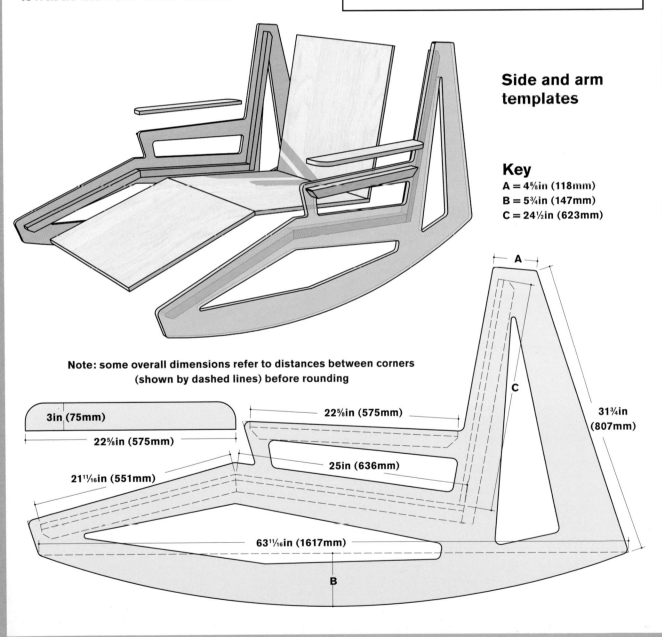

Side and arm templates

Key

A = 4⅝in (118mm)
B = 5¾in (147mm)
C = 24½in (623mm)

Note: some overall dimensions refer to distances between corners (shown by dashed lines) before rounding

3in (75mm)

22⅝in (575mm)

21¹¹⁄₁₆in (551mm)

22⅝in (575mm)

25in (636mm)

31¾in (807mm)

63¹¹⁄₁₆in (1617mm)

Design

1 The first step was to come up with a shape that looked OK and would work. After a few scribblings on paper, I felt the need to draw something out full-size as a rod or template. I could then stand back and see if it made sense. The first thing I wanted to establish was the curve of the rocker profile, using a piece of ply bent into a suitable shape.

2 The next stage was to determine the seat and back angles and mark those out. At this point it was all guesswork, aided by my own experience of creating anatomically acceptable shapes and sizes.

3 Here's the shape mocked up with masking tape on an old sheet of pinboard – though the holes in the pinboard proved to be a bit of a nuisance when it came to drawing and cutting the outline. If I had used plain hardboard, then the template could have been used with a bearing-guided cutter for a smooth result; however, the edges would need to be smooth, and hardboard can become slightly fluffy when cut.

4 However, this was the finished shape I came up with. Every junction or corner was rounded to make it more comfortable and easy on the eye. Now it was time to turn this into a usable template.

5 All the lines were handsawn or jigsawn as neatly as possible so there wouldn't be too much cleaning up to do.

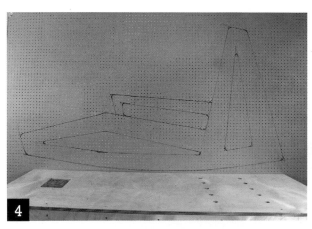

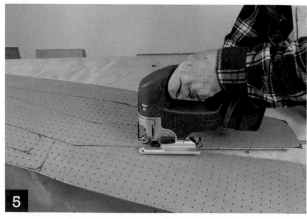

6 This was, in theory, the finished shape – although the rocker curve wasn't smooth enough and still needed some further adjustment.

7 Some cleaning up with my restored vintage block plane was necessary to make the edges as even as possible.

8 A fine-cut rasp dealt with the rough internal corners so they would look even and consistent all the way round.

Making the sides

9 Now to mark out both sides of the recliner on a sheet of ⅝in (15mm) ply. I wanted to minimize waste, although some was inevitable. However, I figured that by careful cutting out, I could save most of it for later use.

10 The first step was to climb on my very solid bench top with a mini circular saw and guide rail, and use this as a plunge saw to make the basic separation cuts. This would reduce the board into usable pieces and make it easier to work with. I had a tripod support for the board where it overhung the bench.

11 The shorter cuts were done with a conventional handsaw and a Japanese pullsaw, working close to the lines. The external corners would be trimmed with a jigsaw.

12 Internal corner cuts were done with the jigsaw and scroll-cutting blade, then the straight cuts in between were made with a handsaw.

13 After some cleaning up with the rasp, here's one side finished – just one more to do and there would be a matching pair.

14 Any gaps in the edges of the ply were filled with wood filler and smoothed off, so that when the edges were routed, the cutter bearing had something to run against. Here, I used a ⅛in (3.2mm) roundover bit in a trimmer, which made edge moulding quick and fuss-free.

15 Now that I had my matching pair of side profiles, the rest of the construction would, in theory, be quite straightforward.

Seat, back, arms and footrest

16 The seat and back are simply two boards with 1¼in (32mm) square PAR softwood glued along each side. The arms of the chair use the same simple method.

17 Before assembly I decided to use my sanding 'bat' to smooth all the rounded edges, using 80 mesh to ensure the edges were fully rounded.

18 The radiused ends of the arms were bandsawn roughly, then shaped carefully on a disc sander, which helped to create nice curves.

19 All visible sections of the softwood were rounded over with the ⅛in (3.2mm) roundover cutter to make their touch and appearance more pleasing. The panel for the footrest was made in the same way as the back and seat, with softwood strips down each side. However, because of the meeting angle with the seat, the ends of the strips needed to be trimmed at an angle so as to fit closely together.

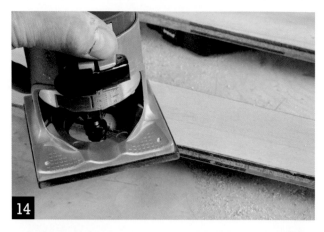
14

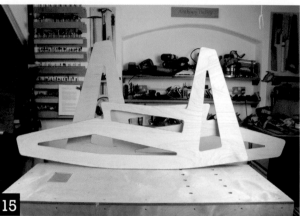
15

16

17

18

19

20 The same rounding-over treatment was given to all the exposed edges, which were then smoothed with an abrasive pad.

Assembly

21 A combined drill and countersink was used to make the holes for 'honest' visible screw fixings in the side pieces. These would fix the seat and back in position.

22 Once the seat was screwed in place, the whole thing became rigid enough to work on. The back was positioned to meet the seat below it. The design was intended from the start to allow for cushions about 3½–4in (90–100mm) thick. They would be held in place but visible from the side.

23 The arms were simply screwed in place flush with the top of the side profiles. None of the components that fit between the sides are glued to them; screws alone give enough rigidity and strength.

24 Those rocker curves were still giving a bit of bother because there were still flat spots where the recliner would quickly come to rest, so some extra hand-planing and checking by eye was needed to get the curvature exactly right.

25 The completed recliner now looks the part, and with some cushions in place it becomes a very comfortable, relaxing place to sit. The finish is up to you. This project would look good painted – black, for example, would create a striking effect with contrasting cushions.

BRIDLE-JOINT STOOL

This traditional rustic-style oak stool has a frame constructed using bridle joints, and a top that is edge-jointed. By varying the proportions, the design could be stretched longways to make a coffee table or upwards to create a hall stand.

Cutting list

Hardwood such as oak, chestnut or ash
Seat (joined from 2 pieces)   1 @ 12¾ x 12¾ x 1in
(325 x 325 x 25mm)
Legs 4 @ 19¾ x 1½ x 1½in (500 x 38 x 38mm)
Stretchers and seat rails 5 @ 11¾ x 1½ x 1½in
(300 x 38 x 38mm)

What you need

- Timber per cutting list
- Handsaw
- Tenon saw
- Jack or fore plane
- Smoothing plane
- Block plane
- Marking gauge
- Mortise gauge
- Try-square
- Roofing square
- Marking knife
- ½in (12.7mm) square-edged (firmer) chisel
- Wide bevel-edged chisel
- PVA glue
- Beeswax polish or pure beeswax
- Hot-air gun

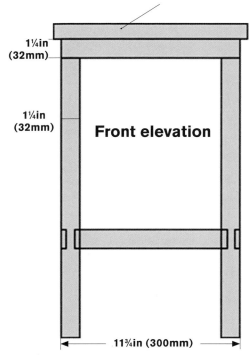

Bridle-jointed top

1¼in
(32mm)

1¼in
(32mm)

Front elevation

11¾in (300mm)

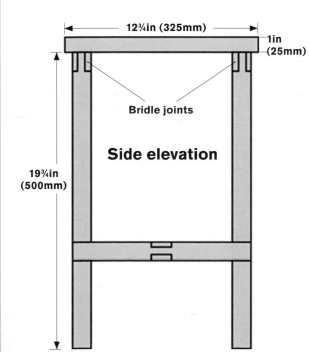

12¾in (325mm)

1in
(25mm)

Bridle joints

Side elevation

19¾in
(500mm)

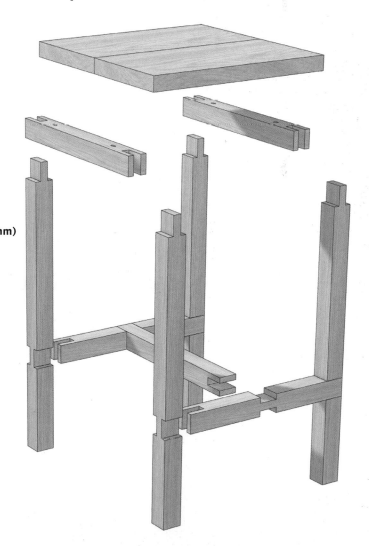

Exploded view

Timber preparation

1 With the wood thoroughly acclimatized to your workshop environment, and after removing any cracked ends from the timber, start by marking and measuring out the legs and rails from 1½in (38mm) stock. Cut this to a square section.

2 Now plane the reference face on it. The legs and rails for this project are all made from material of the same cross section.

3 Pressing the stock of the marking gauge against the reference face, mark the thickness of the planed components to 1¼in (32mm) and use a try-square to set the two adjoining surfaces accurately at right angles. Angling the plane while smoothing has the benefit of shearing awkward grain more effectively and, by varying the angle, you can often avoid tearing. However, bear in mind that angling also reduces the plane's effective length. This means that the guaranteed straightness of the surface also reduces, so while this technique is acceptable for short legs and rails, it is no use for example while edge-jointing, where maximum straightness is required.

Marking the bridle joints

The bridle joint is a type of mortise and tenon. The socket or mortise takes the form of an open-sided slot, while the peg or tenon has shoulders on only two sides. The marking consists of the knifed shoulder line that runs around the timber and the gauged lines for the cheeks that run along and across the end. The lines are marked in the same positions for both the peg and the socket.

4 To avoid accumulating errors from measurement, the width of a joint is marked directly from the corresponding piece with a knife line to show where the shoulders and the socket base will be. Make a nick in the wood to mark the position, and then insert the knife tip in the nick and slide a try-square up against the knife before running the blade along the square's edge to make the line.

5 A mortise gauge with two marking spurs is convenient for this type of joint because you can set the width and the position of the mortise independently. The same gauge settings are used for the pins and sockets of the bridle joint. The convention with this type of joint is for the lines of the cheeks to divide the thickness of the wood into three, so the peg will be one third of the width and the two sides of the socket will form the other two thirds. For improved strength, I chose to increase the thickness of the peg slightly to ½in (12.7mm); this corresponds to a standard (imperial) chisel size, which is handy for chopping out the socket.

6 The joint is positioned in the centre of the wood. It is important to note here that the stock is pressed against the corresponding faces of both pieces of wood forming the joint. That way, if the positioning of the joint does happen to be slightly off-centre, it will still fit correctly without creating stepped surfaces.

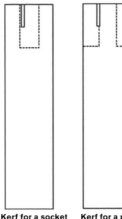

Kerf for a socket   **Kerf for a peg**

Cutting the joints

7 With the marking lines in the same position for both the peg and the socket, the saw cut, or kerf, must always run along the waste side of the line. For the socket cheeks, this means the kerf is to the inside of the line, while for the cheeks of the pegs the kerf is outside the line.

8 Rather than a bevel-edged chisel, use a square-sided (firmer) type to chop out the base of the socket, so it does not have delicate corners that would be easily damaged, and so that its sides register in between the cheeks, holding it square. The socket bases are chopped out with a succession of V-shaped chippings, keeping the base about ¹⁄₃₂in (1mm) inside the line. This allows you to pare away the final slice for a crisp, undented edge.

9 The T-shaped bridle joints where the stretchers meet have the same design of socket, but the pins are formed partway along the legs, where the timber must be reduced in section. Make saw cuts down to the gauge lines, keeping the saw level so it just meets the line on each side.

10 With the wood securely clamped, the waste is chopped away across the grain using a broad chisel. As the recess approaches the gauge line, make finer and finer chops, finally paring halfway across the base of the recess.

11 Turn the wood around and pare from the other side, then turn it over to saw and chop out the recess from the opposite face.

Fitting the joints

The stool frame is first assembled as two H-frame shapes, formed by a pair of legs and a side stretcher between them. Once they are glued and set, the top rails then join the H-frames and the central cross-stretcher to become an A-shaped frame when viewed from the other angle.

12 To test them, all the joints are dry-fitted without using glue. You should aim for joints that fit directly from the saw cut, the main reason being that this drastically reduces the time taken and helps you get projects finished. However, do not force tight joints together, as this will either split the wood immediately or build in stress so that it splits later. Paring away the cheeks and shoulders of a tight joint can still give first-class results, but it requires great care and patience as well as a very sharp chisel.

13 PVA glue is brushed into the sockets so that when the pin is inserted, glue is pushed into the joint. If you were to glue the surface of the pin, this would be scraped off as it was inserted into the socket, resulting in a dry joint and a messy surface.

14 Use a flat reference surface for assembly of the components and frames, and a large try-square or roofer's square to check that the joints are right-angled. Make sure no glue dribbles onto your reference surface, or wipe it off immediately if it does. Small beads of glue exuding from the closed joint can be left to chisel off when set, in preference to rubbing them into the wood's surface.

15 When the joints are thoroughly set, clamp the frame in a vice and, using a finely set smoothing plane with a razor-sharp blade, shave across the joints to bring the surfaces flush. Do not shave off the edge of a frame that includes end grain unless you have chamfered this first. Planing across joints on a finished frame can be challenging because of the differing grain directions, but with care it will show your finished joints at their best.

The seat top

The top is a square board made by butt- or edge-jointing two pieces together. If the boards have been quartersawn – the end grain will show the annual growth rings at right angles to the face – they will stay flat. Otherwise, arrange the boards so the growth rings curve in opposite directions. That way any subsequent cupping of the two halves will tend to cancel out.

16 With the boards clamped face to face in a vice, plane both edges together ready for jointing.

17 Check that the edges meet accurately by flipping one board over and standing the two pieces edge to edge with a bright light behind. Any glimmer between the edges means further planing is needed. If gaps are forming towards the ends of the joint, this means the plane is rocking lengthways and more care is needed to press on the front knob at the start of each stroke and the rear tote or handle at the end of the stroke.

18 When no light is visible, the two sides of the top can be glued and clamped together.

Attaching the top

When a flat top is fixed to a frame, there is often a conflict of grain direction with potential for stress to the frame or splitting of the top. Furniture makers have various means of dealing with this, but one of the simplest is to screw the top through slotted holes in the frame.

19 The slots in the upper rails of the frame run at right angles to the direction of the grain in the top. Allow for a 2% movement in the wood so, if the screws are 8in (200mm) apart, make the slots ⁵⁄₃₂in (4mm) wider than the screws. The screws are waxed and fully tightened, then released slightly to allow movement in the slot if tension arises.

The finished stool

20 A micro-bevel shaved with a block plane can be used to avoid leaving a delicate sharp edge or arris that can easily splinter. Apply this technique all over to make the finished furniture feel and look more friendly, as well as avoiding the risk of disputes with injured users.

21 Beeswax finish is very traditional and one of the quickest, simplest and cheapest ways to provide oak furniture with a lasting warm glow. It repels dirt and creates a silky surface which, while not durable, is easily maintained and improves with age. Either use a proprietary beeswax paste, or you can apply pure beeswax without solvents if you warm the wooden surface using a hot-air gun. Rub the block of wax against the wood and as it turns to liquid, allow some seconds for it to soak in, then wipe away the excess with a cotton rag. Ensure there are no solidified dribbles left, especially where they could end up caked on clothing, then rub the surface to a final sheen with a fresh cotton rag.

SOLITAIRE BOARD

Solitaire is one of those traditional games that are enduring and easy to play – but also rather easy to lose at. Making a solitaire board is also a challenge. The biggest poser was how to create rows of evenly spaced recesses for the marbles.

Solitaire is just that – a solitary game that requires one player only. The centre marble is removed and each leapfrog move may be made vertically or horizontally. The trick is to remove all the marbles to complete the game successfully. There is a skill in doing this and thus winning against yourself. You can buy packs of marbles either in a games or toyshop or online. Most boards are round: I couldn't see a problem with mine being octagonal, however. I also wanted to make it visually a little more interesting by edge-gluing some contrasting woods together.

What you need

- Offcuts of two contrasting hardwoods, e.g. ash and walnut
- 33 glass marbles
- Plywood offcuts for hole-spacing template, etc.
- Planer-thicknesser or bench plane
- Pillar drill with ¾in (20mm) sawtooth Forstner bit
- Router with ⅝in (16mm) corebox cutter
- ¾in (20mm) guide bush, used with both of the above cutters
- Router table
- Cordless drill with ball-ended abrasive bit
- Block plane
- Mitre square
- Random orbital sander
- Sanding block
- Wax oil
- Baize or felt if desired

Plan

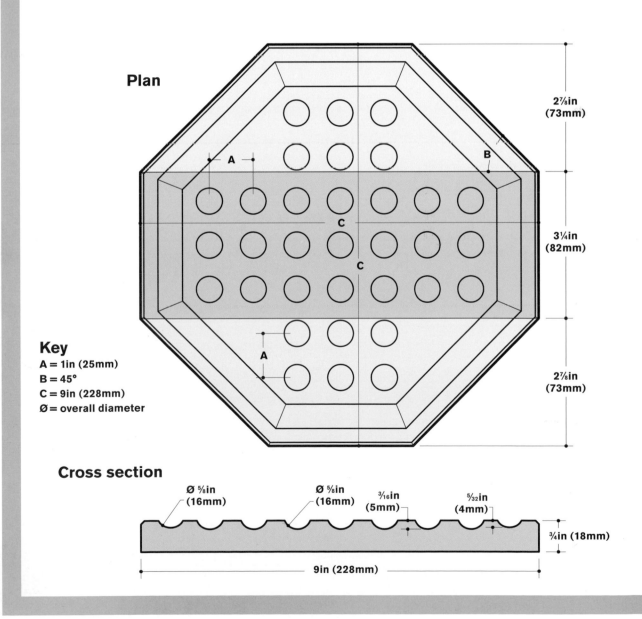

2⅞in (73mm)

3¼in (82mm)

2⅞in (73mm)

Key

A = 1in (25mm)
B = 45°
C = 9in (228mm)
Ø = overall diameter

Cross section

Ø ⅝in (16mm)
Ø ⅝in (16mm)
³⁄₁₆in (5mm)
⁵⁄₃₂in (4mm)
¾in (18mm)

9in (228mm)

1 The first job was to thickness and edge some offcuts – two pieces of ash (*Fraxinus excelsior*) and one of walnut (*Juglans regia*) – and glue them together using my incredibly useful bench dogs to clamp them tight. I have two wide strips of planed softwood which I use to safely and comprehensively clamp anything between the dogs, and they also act as spacers if needed.

2 I considered using the router table to machine the recesses with a ⅝in (16mm) corebox cutter. However, as I would not be able to see what was happening, getting exact spacing could be a hideous exercise. So I decided to make an 'overhand' jig by drilling spaced holes for a ¾in (20mm) guide bush in a piece of ¼in (6mm) birch ply. The holes' centres were at 1in (25mm) intervals in three rows of seven.

3 A ¾in (20mm) sawtooth Forstner bit proved to be an exact sliding fit with the chosen guide bush. The pillar drill I used has a new sub-table fence and clamp fitted. On this I put a piece of birch ply as a sacrificial board. By aligning the point of the Forstner on each cross line, I found I could get very precisely spaced drill holes.

4 The new jig needed de-fluffing but apart from that it was ready to go. I did consider whether it needed a fence to run off, but as I was using odd-sized offcuts that wasn't a workable option. In fact, at this point, I realized this project wasn't going to be as difficult as most of mine to execute!

5 I found the 'working centre' of the workpiece – the place where I knew there was enough wood all round if I chopped the corners off. Then perpendicular cross lines were drawn, centred on the middle, walnut section. These would be my aiming lines for setting the jig in place.

6 Thin veneer pins were used at the corners to hold the jig in position. Since the corners were going to be chopped off, these tiny holes would go anyway. The jig was sighted and centred on the middle row of holes.

7 With the ¾in (20mm) guide bush and ⅝in (16mm) corebox cutter installed, the router was rested in one of the holes and, while static, the cutter was plunged to touch the board blank. The depth gauge was then set for about ³⁄₁₆in (5mm) deep. This was experimental, as the recess needed to be just

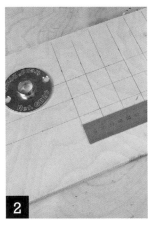

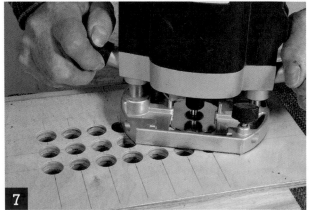

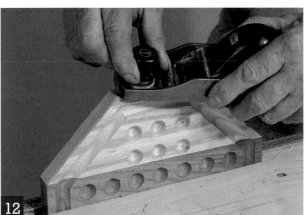

deep enough to locate each marble. Once I had found what looked like a suitable depth, I stuck with that throughout. Each recess was plunged and cut in turn. Then the jig was lifted and turned perpendicular to the first set of recesses, using the other pencilled centre line. It was then pinned in place and the remaining recesses machined. The nine centre holes, of course, were already done.

8 The recesses were now all machined but a little rough on the inside, so I used a ball-ended abrasive bit in a cordless drill to give a completely smooth finish.

9 Now the corners could be chopped off at 45°. I decided to make these edges longer because it looked better when they exactly met the edge of the walnut centre strip. This wouldn't affect the recesses at all, or the running recess around the outside of the board.

10 Once the shape was cut out, I needed to machine the running recess. To do this, I drew two pencil lines on the router table sub-fence that lined up with the diameter of the same corebox cutter, now fitted in the table. I lined up the corner of each edge with the start pencil line and did a 'drop-on' cut. When the stop pencil line was reached, I lifted the wood off at the back end.

11 The running recesses met surprisingly well at each corner, which was a relief!

12 I decided to keep all the board edges square but applied a tiny bevel on all the arrises around the upper face. I could have used a bearing-guided bevel cutter in the router table but I opted instead for a block plane, as it was quick and easy to do. The only proviso was to work only with, not against, the grain to avoid tearout.

13 A good sanding was now required. The edges were completed using a sanding block. The recesses had already been sanded.

14 My favourite finish is wax oil, which I applied liberally, using kitchen paper to wipe out all the excess before leaving the board to dry. If you'd like to apply a final finishing touch, simply affix some baize or felt underneath – otherwise, it's 'game on'.

SHOVE-HALFPENNY BOARD

Here's another traditional board game – this time a highly competitive one that has been played for many years. It's low-tech fun for all ages.

The idea of shove-halfpenny (pronounced 'haype-nee') is to place a coin on the near end of the board, overhanging the edge, and then shove it with your hand so that it slides up the board, ideally stopping between two of the marked lines. Any coin of around 1in (25mm) diameter will do.

What you need

- One plank, preferably hardwood
- Saw
- Biscuit joiner (optional)
- Clamps
- Random orbital sander
- Abrasives to 240 grit
- Dividers
- Router with 1/16in (1.5mm) inlay cutter
- 1/16in (1.5mm) stained boxwood inlay line
- Block plane if needed
- Hammer
- Cabinet scraper
- Jigsaw
- Danish oil
- Hard wax

Key
A = 1/16in (1.5mm)
B = 15/16in (23mm)
C = 1 3/16in (30mm)
Ø = overall diameter

Plank

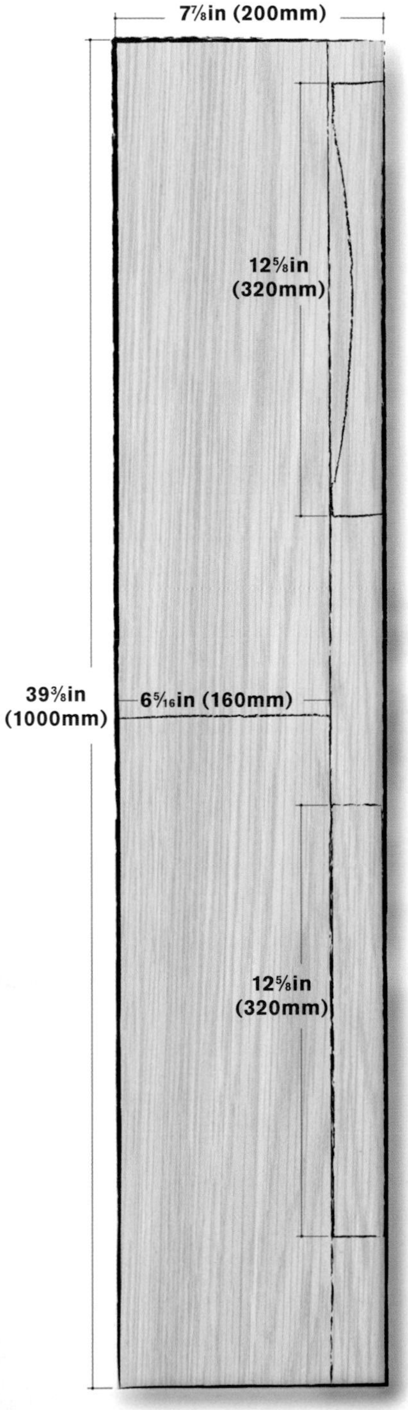
7⅞in (200mm)
12⅝in (320mm)
39⅜in (1000mm)
6 5/16in (160mm)
12⅝in (320mm)

Board

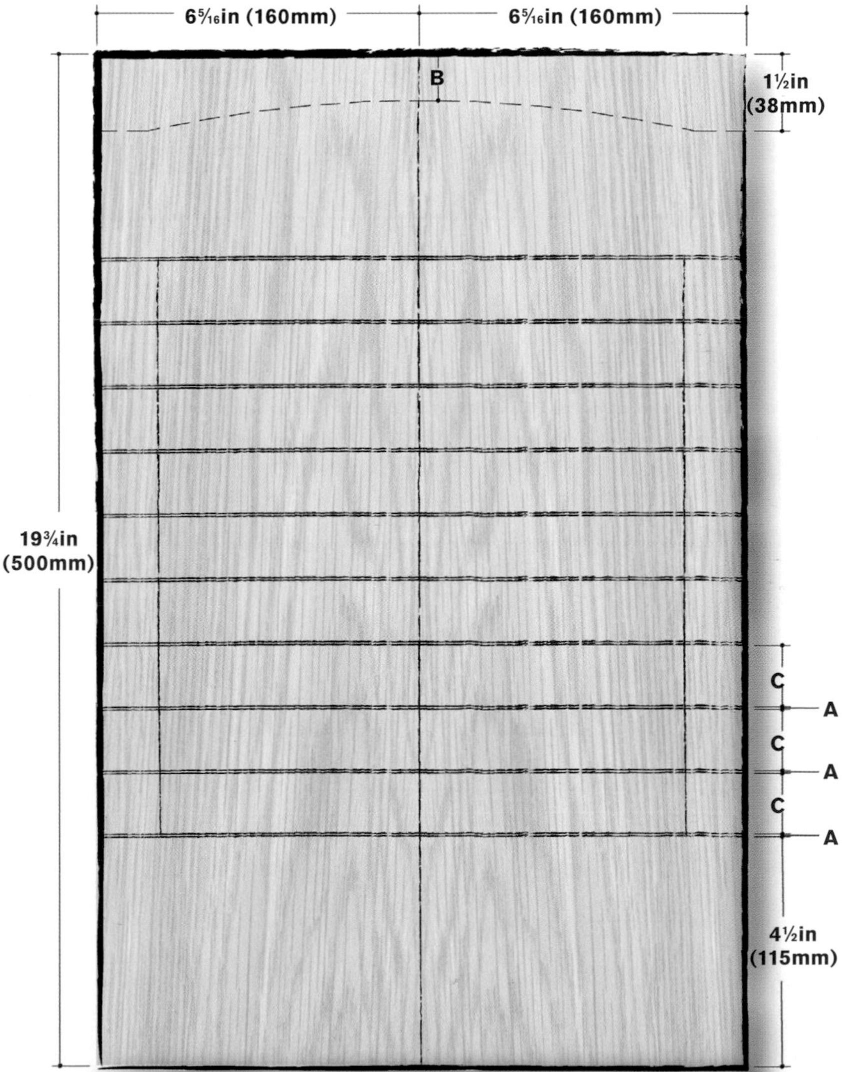
6 5/16in (160mm)
6 5/16in (160mm)
B
1½in (38mm)
19¾in (500mm)
C
A
C
A
C
A
4½in (115mm)

1 Choose a good-quality hardwood; I used English oak (*Quercus robur*). Take a board roughly 40 x 8in (1000 x 200mm), rip off 1½in (40mm) for the end pieces, and then cut it in half. Take the two halves and arrange side by side so that the growth rings are running in opposite directions.

2 Plane the edges to ensure a good joint. If you plan to use biscuits, mark out their positions on both sides of the joint line.

3 Cut the joints with your biscuit joiner…

4 … then apply glue and insert the biscuits.

5 Clamp the boards up tight and leave to cure.

6 Remove the board from the clamps and smooth the surface. Remove any spots of glue and use a random orbital sander, moving through the grits down to 240, which will produce a fine finish. The finished board must be perfectly smooth so the coins can slide easily.

7 Now mark out the positions for the inlay lines. The first one is set 4½in (115mm) from the front edge, there is a gap of 1³⁄₁₆in (30mm) between each, and there are ten lines. Marking out offers endless possibilities for mistakes, so try to simplify it. The gap between each pair of marked lines should be 1¼in (31.5mm) to take account of the thickness of the inlay line. Use a pair of dividers set to this measurement to mark the spacings at each end of the lines.

8 Here's a close-up of the ¹⁄₁₆in (1.5mm) inlay cutter and the inlay lines, which are made from stained boxwood.

9 Fit the cutter in your router and stand it on a level surface with the power disconnected. Gently plunge the router down so the tip of the cutter is just touching the surface. Now take a piece of the inlay line and sandwich it between the adjusting rod and the turret on the base of the router. Lock the rod in this position, and you have now set the correct depth of cut.

10 Routing the grooves is not difficult, but you must have a secure guide. A guide-clamp is ideal, but failing that, a straight batten clamped across the board will be fine. Run the router at full speed and make sure to keep it pressed hard against the batten or guide. Move the router very slowly to avoid stressing the cutter.

11 You may need to clean out the grooves with a piece of folded abrasive paper, and then gently sand the whole surface to remove any pencil marks, or any scratches left by the router.

12 It is a fiddly job inserting the inlay. Being made of timber, it is invariably an irregular size and may need to be adjusted. You can use abrasive paper or a block plane, and once you have got it down to size, apply a few drops of glue to the groove and use a hammer to gently tap the line into place.

13 Once the lines are installed, it is not possible to sand the surface any more. If you do, the black dust from the inlay will contaminate the surrounding timber, turning it all grey. To clean up the top, use a cabinet scraper which produces shavings rather than dust.

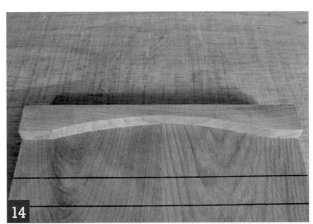

14 Take the 1½in (40mm) timber offcut you ripped off at the beginning, and make a header plate for the top of the board. This is simply a buffer to catch any coins that overshoot. Cut a gentle curve in the centre with a jigsaw and sand the whole thing off.

15 The final job is to attach a batten from your ripped offcut across the underside of the board, about 2in (50mm) in from the front edge. This will locate the board on the edge of a table so that it can't slide about during play.

16 Before finishing, go round the board with abrasive and round over all the corners and edges so that they are soft to the touch.

17 Apply your chosen finish – Danish oil was used here. Three or four thin coats followed by a layer of hard wax should provide the ideal playing surface.

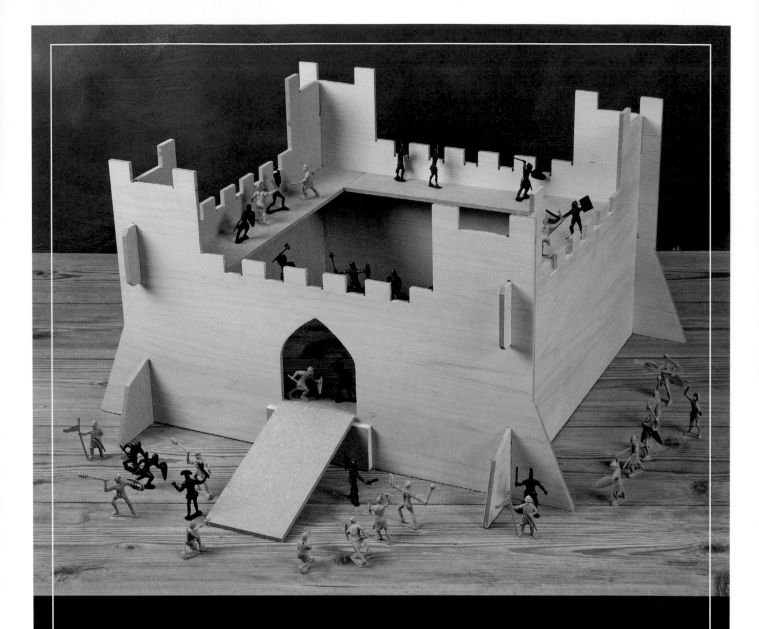

CASTLE

This perennially popular toy can be slotted together and taken apart, and is scaled to match the small knight figures that can be bought inexpensively from most toyshops.

This project uses ¼in (6mm) MDF or ply throughout, which can be either sealed or painted when complete.

Key
A = ¼in (6mm)
B = ¾in (20mm)
C = 1in (26mm)
D = 1³⁄₁₆in (30mm)
E = 2⅜in (60mm)
F = 2¹¹⁄₁₆in (68mm)
G = 2¾in (70mm)
H = 2¹⁵⁄₁₆in (75mm)
J = 3⅛in (80mm)

What you need

- ¼in (6mm) MDF or ply for walls, walkway and drawbridge
- ¾in (20mm) square batten to support the walkway
- Bandsaw
- Handsaw
- Cordless drill
- Jigsaw
- Router with ¼in (6.4mm) straight bit
- Straightedge or router T-square
- Wood file

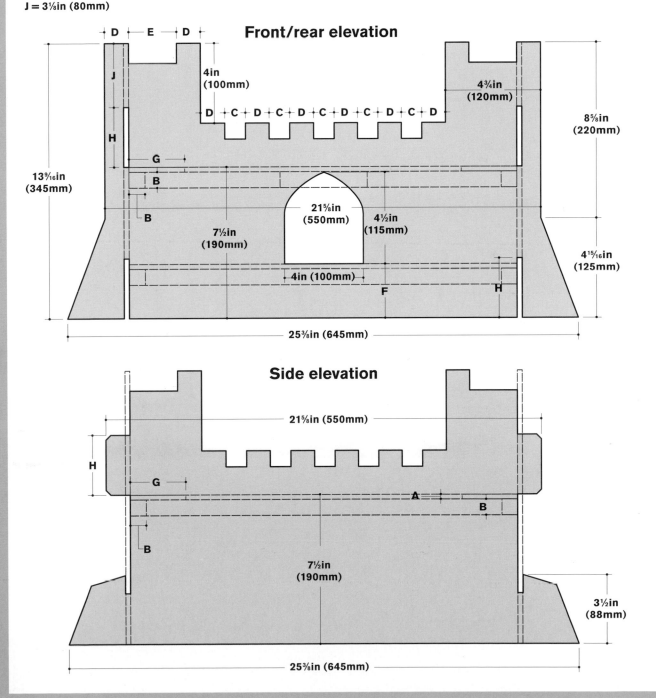

Front/rear elevation

Side elevation

1 Cutting the board out oversize at first makes it easier to handle.

2 Carefully lay out the design using the plan as a guide. If you already have the knight figures, you can check that the design looks in scale with them.

3 A bandsaw is the easy way to cut out the towers and crenellations. However, you need to be a bit ingenious with your cuts, including marking the reverse face as well so you can get under the bandsaw guides for all the cuts.

4 Carefully nibble out the bottom of each crenellation. Don't worry if the cuts aren't perfectly straight: castles cannot always have been in perfect order, especially after a few assaults by the enemy!

5 Drill an entry hole for the jigsaw so you can cut the arch shape. This is quite wide to allow for plenty of fighting underneath the imagined portcullis.

6 Try and get a nice symmetrical arch profile when cutting, and tidy the shape with a wood file afterwards.

7 The front elevation should look something like this. Get this front wall right and you can use it as a template for the other three sides.

8 Mark out two slots that will allow the sides to clip together. The board is a fraction under ¼in (6mm) thick and the router cutter will be exactly ¼in (6.4mm), which gives just enough movement without binding.

9 Use a straightedge or router T-square to make both through slots. Keep them the same on both the back and front walls.

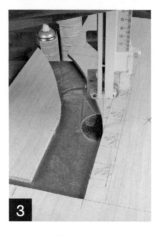

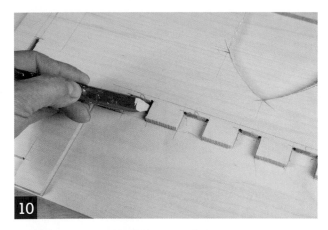

10 Now draw out the other three walls using the front one as the template. You can tidy the lines once the template is lifted off.

11 The adjoining side walls are different because they need a buttress shape at the bottom which has a short slot for the front and back walls to hook into and a tab above which pushes through the upper routed slot. This will hold the castle walls together.

12 The tab at the top will need trimming to get a good firm fit in the slot, but the resultant joints should look like this one. Mark all the joints so you know which goes where. These marks can be sanded off later and more discreet marking applied instead.

13 A small pad is glued on the front of the castle for the drawbridge support.

14 Lengths of ¾in (20mm) square batten are glued inside the walls to support the walkways along the ramparts. Their position should allow knights to see and aim weapons through the crenels (the openings in the battlements).

15 With the ramp in place, the last job is to glue in the walkways behind the battlements. Let battle commence!

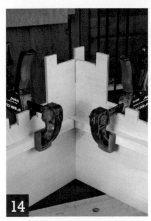

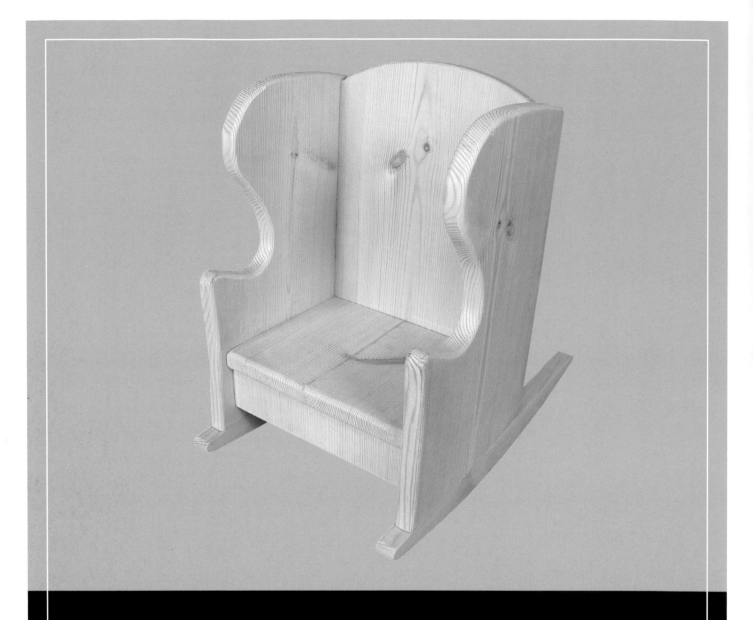

TOY ROCKING CHAIR

This cosy little rocker makes the perfect chair for an average-sized teddy, but there is no reason why you could not scale up the components to suit a child.

Drawing out the curved sides for this piece can be a bit of a challenge. An easy method is to take a large piece of paper and draw some experimental curves freehand. When you find a shape you like, transfer it onto the timber by scribbling on the back face of the paper under the curve. Lay the paper on the timber right way up and trace along the curve again, and it should transfer onto the timber.

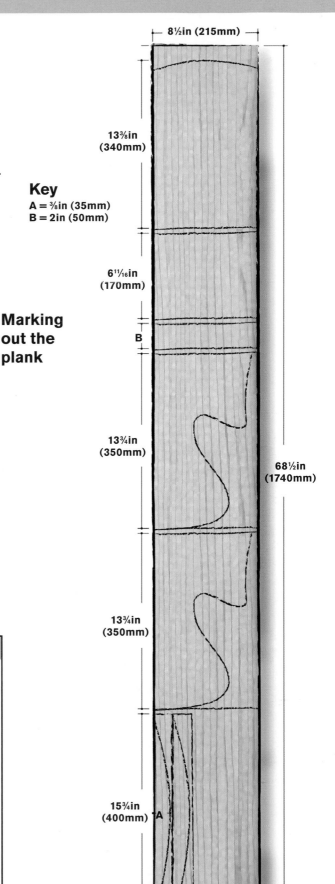

Key
A = ⅜in (35mm)
B = 2in (50mm)

Marking out the plank

8½in (215mm)

13⅜in (340mm)

6¹¹⁄₁₆in (170mm)

B

13¾in (350mm)

68½in (1740mm)

13¾in (350mm)

15¾in (400mm)   A

What you need

- One softwood plank, 1in (25mm) nominal thickness, marked out as shown
- Tablesaw
- Bandsaw
- Jigsaw or coping saw
- Palm, drum and disc sanders
- Biscuit joiner
- Measuring/marking kit
- Router table with bearing-guided roundover cutter
- Pocket-screw jig
- Drill
- Block plane
- Clamps
- Glue
- Child-safe finish of your choice

1 Mark out your plank according to the drawing on page 159.

2 Crosscut the two side panels to length.

3 Clamp both sides together and cut out the curve with a jigsaw or coping saw.

4 The sides cut out.

5 However good your cutting, the edges will still need smoothing. Use a drum sander on the internal curve.

6 A palm sander is good for the external curve.

7 The chair needs to sit at an angle on the rockers. Mark a point 1in (25mm) up from the rear corner of the side piece and then draw a line from the front corner up to this point.

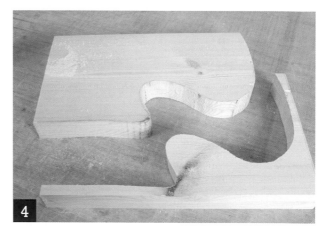

8 You can cut both pieces at the same time by stacking them on the tablesaw and using an angled crosscut fence. Alternatively, you can cut them separately using a handsaw.

9 The curve for the rockers has a radius of 24¾in (620mm). To mark this, you can put a nail in your bench and use either a long rule or a piece of string to draw the curve.

10 Cut the back panel roughly to length and mark a curve across its top. To do this, make a mark on each side 1in (25mm) from the top then, using a piece of string pivoting around the centre of the board, draw a curve through these two points and as close to the top edge as possible.

11 Cut out the rockers using a jigsaw or bandsaw.

12 Clamp both rockers together and smooth them evenly on a belt sander.

13 Round the ends of the rockers on a disc sander.

14 Use the bandsaw again to cut the curve on the top of the back panel.

15 All the components, including the seat and apron, are now cut out and ready for assembly.

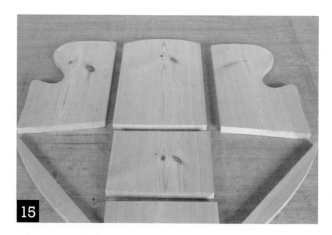

16 Before assembling the chair, the edges of the main components need to be rounded over. Use a bearing-guided cutter mounted in a router table for this.

17 Carefully run the cutter around the front edges of the side panels, the top of the rear panel, the front edge of the seat and the bottom edge of the apron.

18 The back and sides are assembled using biscuit joints. Mark out the positions of the biscuits on both sides of the joint line…

19 …then cut the slots.

20 Apply a little glue to the slots in one component and insert the biscuits, and then apply the glue to the other component's slots.

21 Assemble the back and sides and clamp until dry.

22 The apron is attached to the underside of the seat, again using biscuits. Set it back about ¼in (6mm) from the front edge. Glue and clamp up.

23 The seat is held in position with pocket screws. Use a jig to drill two holes in each side.

24 Slide the seat into position and drive in the screws.

25 The rockers will be joined to the sides using biscuits. To disguise any discrepancies in the joint and also to provide a straight shadow line, use a block plane to form a small chamfer on the bottom edge of each side piece. You can do the same on the outer edge of the rocker.

26 Mark the positions of the biscuits on the sides and the rockers.

27 Cutting the slots for the biscuits.

28 Apply glue to all the joints, assemble and clamp up. Carefully hand-sand the completed chair before applying a child-safe finish of your choice.

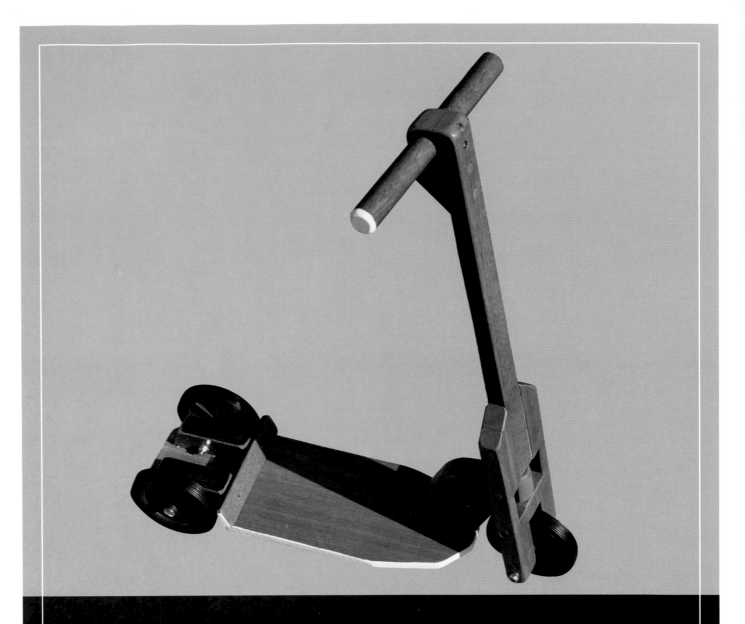

TOY SCOOTER

Whether you build it with two wheels at the back and one in front or vice versa, this scooter is strong and stable in use and suitable for children aged three to four.

What you need

- Hardwood and plywood per cutting list
- Wheels, bolts, cross-dowels and screws as specified under 'Safety first', page 168
- Pillar drill
- Tablesaw, bandsaw or handsaw
- Mitre saw
- Biscuit joiner and size 20 biscuits
- PVA glue
- Low-VOC water-based varnish or paint

Cutting list

Cutting list is for version with two rear wheels
For version with two front wheels, see dimensioned drawings. Use straight-grained hardwood except where ply is specified.

Handlebar
1 @ 9½in x 1in diam. (240mm x 25mm diam.)
Handlebar fixing block
1 @ 3½ x 1½ x 1¼in (90 x 38 x 32mm)

Steering column upright
1 @ 17⅛ x 1¼ x 13/16in (435 x 32 x 20mm)
Outer supports
2 @ 9½ x 1 x ½in (240 x 25 x 12mm)
Top inner supports
2 @ 4½ x 1 x 11/16in (115 x 25 x 17mm)
Bottom inner supports
2 @ 4⅜ x 1 x 11/16in (110 x 25 x 17mm)
Lower block
1 @ 1¼ x 1¼ x 13/16in (32 x 32 x 20mm)
Support extension piece
3 @ 1 3/16 x 1 3/16 x 5/16in (30 x 30 x 8mm)
Upper support block
1 @ 4⅜ x 1 3/16 x 1¼in (110 x 30 x 32mm)
Lower support block
1 @ 5⅜ x 2¾ x 1 3/16in (135 x 70 x 30mm)

Deck (ply)
1 @ 15¾ x 5½ x ½in (400 x 140 x 12mm)
Deck reinforcement (ply)
1 @ 14⅝ x 3½ x ¼in (370 x 90 x 6mm)
Rear wheel supports
2 @ 4⅜ x 1 3/16 x 1¼in (110 x 30 x 32mm)
1 @ 6 x 1 3/16 x ⅝in (150 x 30 x 15mm)

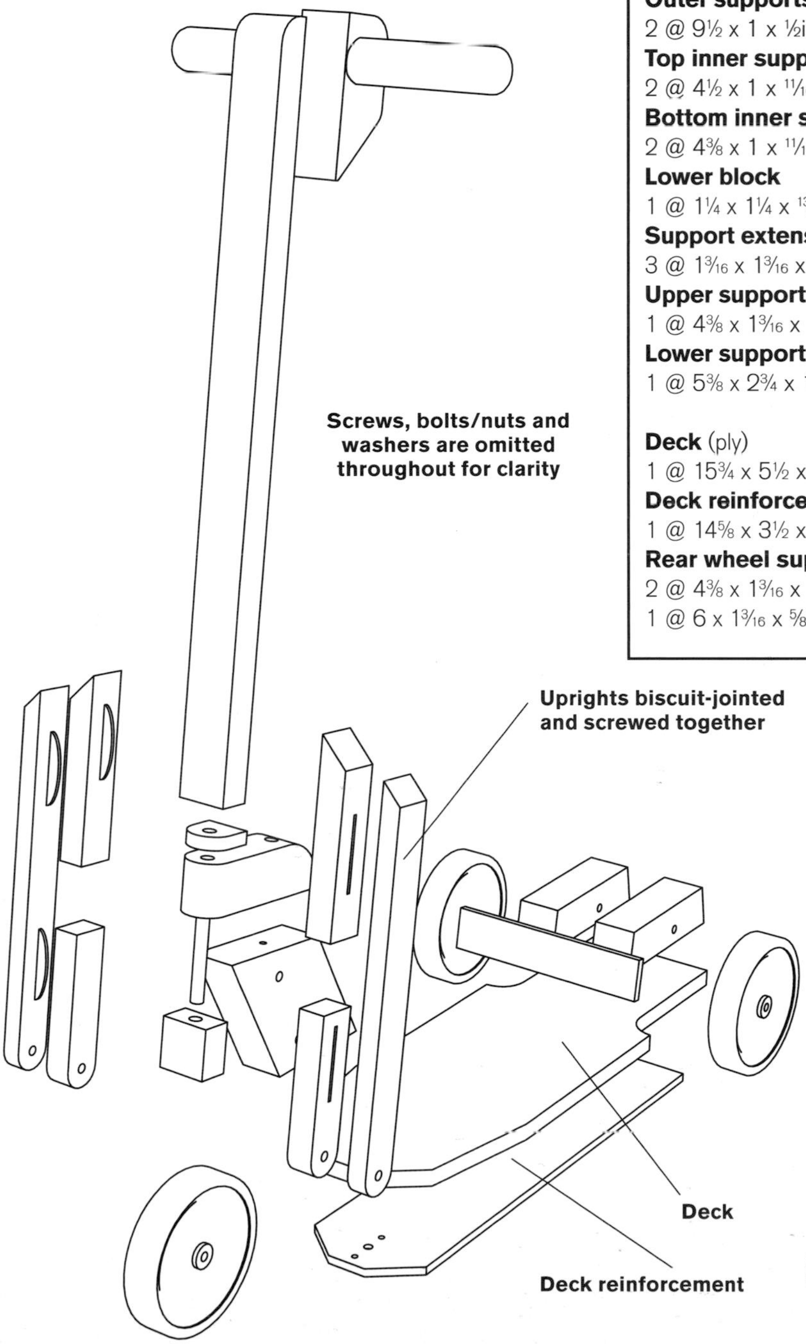

Screws, bolts/nuts and washers are omitted throughout for clarity
Uprights biscuit-jointed and screwed together
Deck
Deck reinforcement

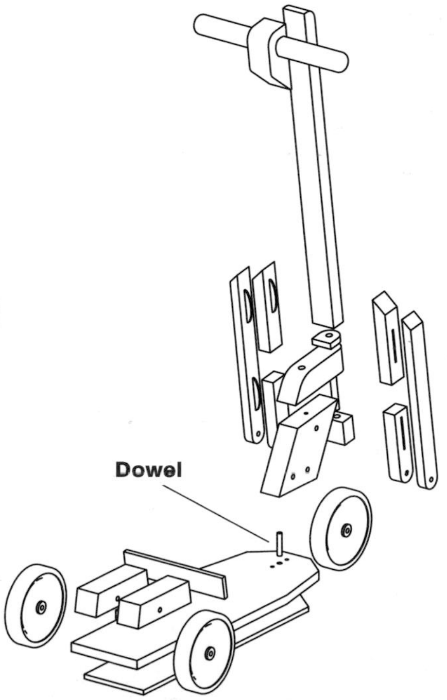

Dowel

Scooters are more popular than they have ever been, with the abundance of youngsters eagerly fizzing along pathways. There has been a particular increase in versions that can be enjoyed by three-year-olds; with parental guidance, these are a useful learning tool for balance and co-ordination. A recent development has been the 'lean and steer' type, with two wheels in the front and one at the back, using a sprung pivotal system. A scooter with two wheels at the back and one in front gives a similar stabilizing effect, but is steered in the normal way.

Side elevation

A = ¼in (6mm)
B = ⁵⁄₁₆in (8mm)
C = ⁷⁄₁₆in (11mm)
D = ¹⁵⁄₃₂in (12mm)
E = ²⁵⁄₃₂in (20mm)
F = 1in (25mm)
G = 1³⁄₁₆in (30mm)
H = 1¼in (32mm)
J = 1¾in (45mm)
K = 3½in (88mm)

Front elevation

A = ¹⁵⁄₃₂in (12mm)
B = ²¹⁄₃₂in (17mm)
C = ²⁵⁄₃₂in (20mm)
D = 1¼in (32mm)
E = 1⅝in (42mm)
F = 4in (102mm)
G = 9⁷⁄₁₆in (240mm)

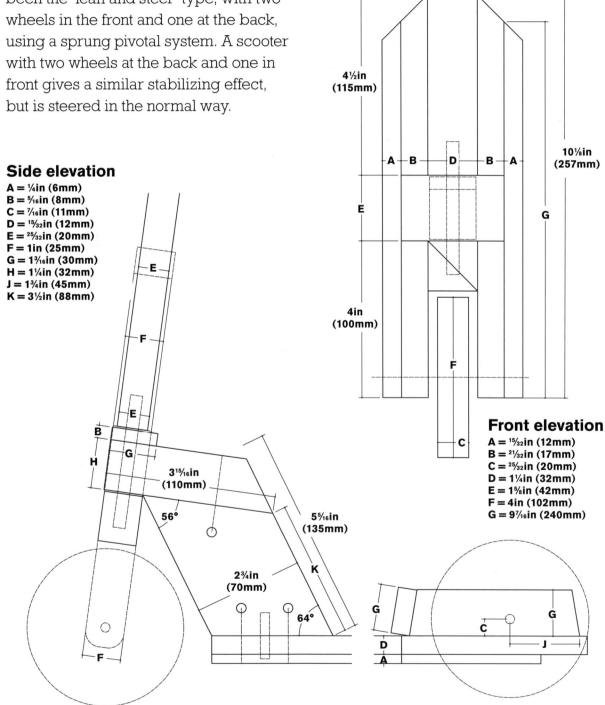

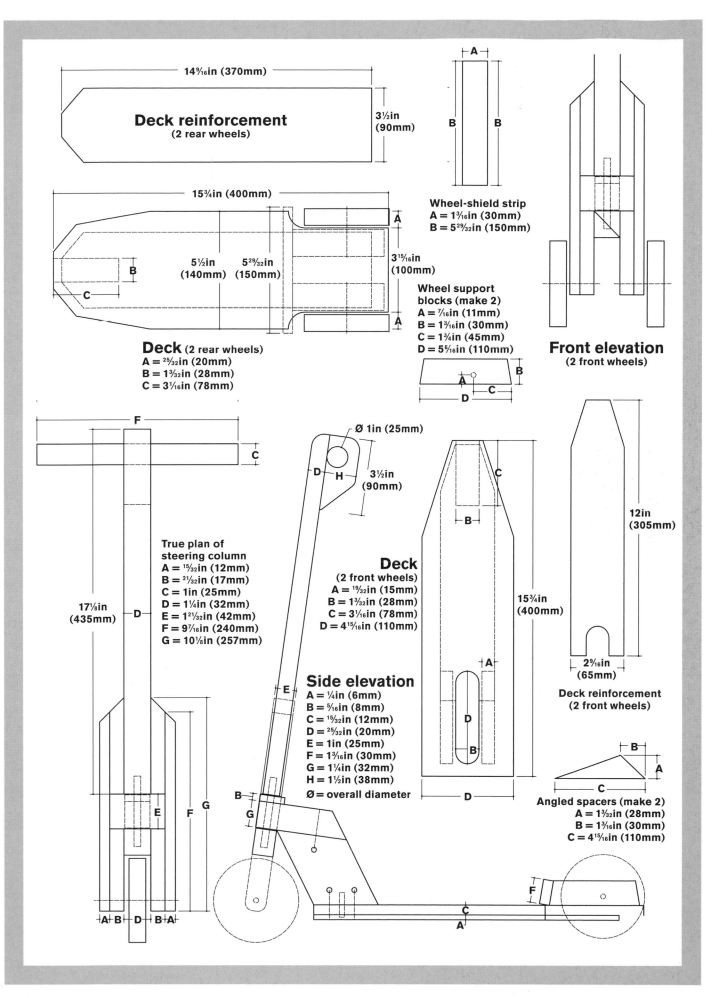

Deck reinforcement
(2 rear wheels)

14⁹⁄₁₆in (370mm)

3½in (90mm)

15¾in (400mm)

5½in (140mm)   5²⁹⁄₃₂in (150mm)

3¹⁵⁄₁₆in (100mm)

A

B

C

A

Deck (2 rear wheels)
A = ²⁵⁄₃₂in (20mm)
B = 1³⁄₃₂in (28mm)
C = 3¹⁄₁₆in (78mm)

A

B   B

Wheel-shield strip
A = 1³⁄₁₆in (30mm)
B = 5²⁹⁄₃₂in (150mm)

Wheel support blocks (make 2)
A = ⁷⁄₁₆in (11mm)
B = 1³⁄₁₆in (30mm)
C = 1¾in (45mm)
D = 5⁵⁄₁₆in (110mm)

B
A
C
D

Front elevation
(2 front wheels)

F

C

17⅛in (435mm)

True plan of steering column
A = ¹⁵⁄₃₂in (12mm)
B = ²¹⁄₃₂in (17mm)
C = 1in (25mm)
D = 1¼in (32mm)
E = 1²¹⁄₃₂in (42mm)
F = 9⁷⁄₁₆in (240mm)
G = 10⅛in (257mm)

D

E
F   G

A B D B A

Ø 1in (25mm)

D   H

3½in (90mm)

Side elevation
A = ¼in (6mm)
B = ⁵⁄₁₆in (8mm)
C = ¹⁵⁄₃₂in (12mm)
D = ²⁵⁄₃₂in (20mm)
E = 1in (25mm)
F = 1³⁄₁₆in (30mm)
G = 1¼in (32mm)
H = 1½in (38mm)
Ø = overall diameter

B

G

C

F

A

Deck
(2 front wheels)
A = ¹⁹⁄₃₂in (15mm)
B = 1³⁄₃₂in (28mm)
C = 3¹⁄₁₆in (78mm)
D = 4¹⁵⁄₁₆in (110mm)

C

B

A

D

B

D

15¾in (400mm)

12in (305mm)

2⁹⁄₁₆in (65mm)

Deck reinforcement
(2 front wheels)

B
A
C

Angled spacers (make 2)
A = 1³⁄₃₂in (28mm)
B = 1³⁄₁₆in (30mm)
C = 4¹⁵⁄₁₆in (110mm)

Safety first

There are important issues that must be addressed when making toys. These relate to the safe practices and materials used to ensure they do not pose a risk to the young user. Essentially, the structure must not use hazardous materials, or have features that can cause injury. All local toy safety regulations must be adhered to if selling or passing on the toy.

These standards have been followed in the construction of the scooters featured in this project. The materials used include plywood and hardwood; all edges have been rounded, and finished with a low-VOC water-based varnish or paint. The screws and other fixing items have had PVA adhesive added to give protection against becoming loose, and wood plugs are used to cover most screw heads. The final nuts used have a nylon insert to reduce the risk of loosening. The steering joint has been limited to ensure that it does not become a finger trap. Having taken all necessary steps to ensure this, it must be stressed that a toy of this type should only be used while there is a responsible adult present, and a safety helmet should be worn. The larger wheels used for this project are 4in (102mm) diameter moulded disc type. They have a hub width of ¾in (20mm) and a bore of ¼in (6.35mm). The rear wheel used in the version with two front wheels is a 2in (50mm) fixed-wheel castor. The spindles used for the moulded wheels are ¼in (M6) bolts.

Cross-dowels are used to secure the front steering column to its support parts, and to the deck. These provide a very strong joint. They require a ¼in (6mm) hole to take the cross-dowel screw and a ⅜in (10mm) hole to take the cross-dowel. It is preferable for the ⅜in (10mm) hole not to be drilled all the way through, for added strength.

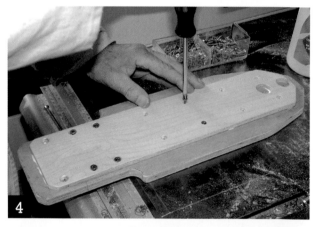

The deck

1 The version with two rear wheels is described first. Begin by cutting the deck blank to size from ½in (12mm) plywood. Then cut out the recesses for the rear wheels, using the pillar drill to form the curved part.

2 A tablesaw can be used to remove the unwanted pieces; alternatively, use a bandsaw or handsaw.

3 Cut the front sides of the blank to a taper. I used the front deck of the mitre saw for this.

4 Cut a reinforcing plate using ¼in (6mm) ply and attach to the bottom of the deck using screws and adhesive. Make sure that the threads of the screws have adhesive on them to reduce the risk of a screw coming loose. The deck can now have its edges painted and varnish applied. Use child-safe water-based finishes.

5 Cut two support blocks for the rear wheels, using a hardwood for strength. Then drill ¼in (6mm) diameter holes to take the wheel spindles.

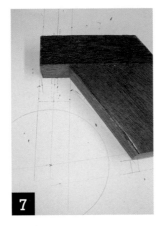

6 Attach the blocks to the top of the deck using adhesive and screws.

Steering column support

7 Cut the components for the steering column support. Use a hardwood for strength and durability.

8 Drill the holes for the cross-dowel bolt and cross-dowel, plus an additional ¼in (6mm) hole for a wooden dowel and one screw hole at the top. Add an extension piece to the front of the support.

9 Drill a ⁵⁄₁₆in (8mm) diameter hole through the front of the support to take the steering spindle. Round over the front, as seen in photo 11.

10 Assemble the front support, using adhesive and one counterbored screw to attach the top piece to the lower piece.

11 Insert a cross-dowel and screw, and tighten firmly using an Allen key. When assembled, soften all edges.

12 Insert a wooden plug to cover the screw head. This method is used with most other visible screws to ensure they will not loosen.

Front forks and steering column

13 Support the central steering upright in a vice or similar, making sure that it is plumb. Drill a ⁵⁄₁₆in (8mm) hole to a depth of 1³⁄₁₆in (30mm) for the steering spindle.

14 Cut the components for the steering column. Cut matching size 20 biscuit slots and additional screw fitting holes. Drill a ⁵⁄₁₆in (8mm) hole centrally in the small lower support block. This, together with the hole drilled in the front steering upright, is used to support the steering spindle.

15 Join the components together using the biscuits and adhesive, and additional screws.

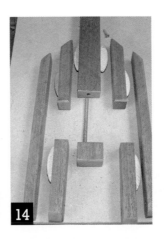

16 Join the final outside components, then cover the screw heads with wooden plugs. The completed assembly can now have a clear acrylic varnish applied. Note that the lower support block is not attached at this stage.

17 Cut the handlebar support to size and use a 1in (25mm) Forstner bit to bore a neat hole. Join to the top of the central steering upright using adhesive and screws.

18 The steering swivel spindle is ⁵⁄₁₆in (8mm) diameter. Use a plain rod if you have one available. Alternatively, use a length of threaded rod and wrap plumbers' PTFE tape around the threads. This will give a better tolerance and provide slight lubricating properties.

19 Place the spindle in position with washers above and below the front end of the steering column support. Engage the spindle in the holes drilled in the bottom of the steering shaft and the lower support block.

20 Push the lower support block firmly so that the front of the steering column support is a snug but free-moving fit. Tighten screws into the block to secure it in this position.

21 The wheel is positioned midway in the gap. Use a ¼ x 4in (M6 x 100mm) roofing bolt with nuts and washers to centralize and secure it. Finish by fitting a nut with a nylon insert.

22 Attach the bottom of the front steering support column to the deck using adhesive and the cross-dowel fixings. In addition, a ¼in (6mm) wood dowel is positioned between the cross-dowel fixings.

Rear wheels

23 The rear wheels use ¼ x 2¾in (M6 x 70mm) bolts as spindles. PTFE tape is again used for lubrication.

24 Feed the remainder of each bolt through the blocks.

25 Secure each wheel spindle in position with nuts and washers, ensuring that the wheel can be rotated with minimal friction. Use a nylon-insert nut and a touch of adhesive to lock the wheel spindle in position.

26 Attach a wheel-shield strip just in front of the rear wheels.

Handlebars

27 Feed a length of 1in (25mm) dowel through the hole bored at the top of the central steering upright, and secure the handlebar with a screw and adhesive. Then just apply finish to the necessary parts (see 'Safety first' information on page 168 for details), and there's your scooter.

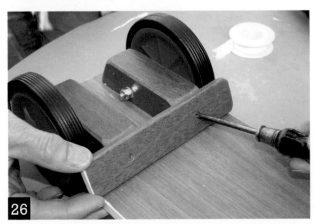

Making a scooter with two front wheels

For this version, the deck is narrower (see drawing on page 167, lower right) and a slot is cut at the rear to take a single wheel. The rear wheel is a 2in (50mm) fixed castor. Alternatively, a larger wheel could be used and mounted through the slot, with support blocks either side. Cut and attach a reinforcing plate to the bottom of the deck as with the other scooter, but making allowances for the single rear wheel.

A The castor is fitted on with angled spacers which are glued, screwed and finally bolted in place, before a thin wooden cover is added.

B The angled spacers allow the wheel to be raised so that the deck is about 1⅜in (35mm) above ground level.

C Attach a wheel to each leg of the front steering column using ¼in (M6) bolts, washers and a nylon-insert nut. Attach the steering column support to the deck using cross-dowel fixings and adhesive.

D And there we have the alternative version complete.

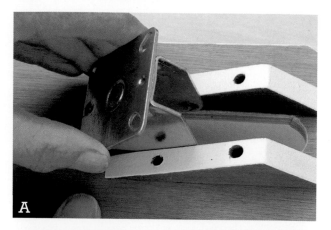

A

B

C

D

GLOSSARY

arris A sharp edge formed where two surfaces meet.

crosscut To saw wood across the grain.

cross-dowel A fixing used for joining two pieces of wood, consisting of a metal cylinder with a threaded hole, inserted across the grain near the end of one component, and a bolt which is passed through the second component and into the cylinder. It is used to avoid driving a screw into the end grain, which would produce a weak joint.

cupped (of timber) Curved across the grain because of uneven moisture loss during seasoning.

datum A point, line or surface which is known to be accurate, from which subsequent measurements are made.

deepsawn (of a board) Sawn through its widest dimension, to produce boards which are the same width as the original piece, but thinner.

featherboard A safety device used with certain woodworking machines, fitted with comb-like, flexible teeth to hold the workpiece flat against the table or fence.

fuming Exposing wood to ammonia fumes to darken its colour. The process is used on woods with a high tannin content, chiefly oak (*Quercus* sp.).

heartwood The harder wood produced near the centre of the tree trunk, as opposed to sapwood, formed in the outer layers of the tree. In some species, sapwood and heartwood differ greatly in colour.

jam chuck (or **jam-fit chuck**) In woodturning, a temporary or improvised chuck made by mounting a piece of scrap wood in the lathe chuck and forming a hole in it into which the workpiece can be tightly fitted (jammed).

kerf The cut made by a saw.

ogee An S-shaped curve.

PAR (of timber) Planed all round; that is, with all four sides planed before sale.

push stick A stick, sometimes fitted with a handle, used to push the workpiece through a woodworking machine so as to keep the user's hands away from the blade.

quartersawn Sawn so that the growth rings in the timber are perpendicular to the surface; this minimizes subsequent warping or distortion of the wood.

resaw To reduce a sawn piece of wood to smaller pieces before making it into individual objects or components.

rip To saw wood along the grain.

rod A template – either literally a rod, or a wider board – on which the lengths of components and the positions of joints are marked for future reference.

sacrificial board An expendable piece of wood which is used to prevent damage to the workpiece, e.g. by placing it underneath a piece to be drilled so that any splintering which occurs damages only the sacrificial piece.

sanding bat A sanding aid consisting of a flat board covered with abrasive paper.

sanding through the grits (or grades) Sanding using progressively finer grades of abrasive, so that each grade removes the scratches made by the previous one.

sapwood The softer wood formed in the outer layers of the growing tree, as opposed to heartwood from nearer the centre of the trunk.

shake A split in wood, caused by trauma, internal stresses or unequal moisture loss.

shoot To plane the edge or end of a piece of wood, often while it is resting on a support called a shooting board.

snipe A rounding over of the ends of a board, caused by allowing the plane to tip at the beginning or end of its stroke.

spelching Splintering of the back edge of a workpiece during sawing or end-grain planing, caused by the pressure of the blade against the unsupported fibres.

stickering Stacking boards to dry with narrow battens (stickers) placed between them to ensure air circulation.

through-and-through or **slabsawing** Sawing a log into parallel slices to minimize wastage. The resulting boards are prone to **cupping** as they dry.

tote The handle of certain tools, such as saws or planes.

VOC Volatile organic compound: an organic chemical, such as formaldehyde, which gives off fumes or vapour that may be harmful to health.

waney-edged Incorporating part of the natural surface of the tree, often including the bark.

CONTRIBUTORS

GMC Publications would like to thank the following contributors for their inspirational projects:

Amber Bailey Marquetry coaster (page 18); **Anthony Bailey** Classic chopping board (page 8), Butler's Tray (page 24), Beer crate (page 39), Wine rack (page 45), Letter rack with drawer (page 70), Mini chest of drawers (page 75), Pigeonhole rack (page 80), Recliner (page 134), Solitaire board (page 146); **Mark Baker and Emma Kennedy** Natural-edge chopping board (page 12); **John Bullar** Bridle-joint stool (page 140); **Fred and Julie Byrne** Mug tree (page 34), Jewellery tree (page 84), Scrollsaw key holder (page 110); **Walter Hall** Rustic stools (page 119); **James Hatter** Toy scooter (page 164); **Derek Jones** Toast rack (page 30); **Kevin Ley** Spoon rack (page 98); **Matt Long** Kitchen bench (page 125); **Mike Mahoney** Turned platter (page 14); **Charles Mak** Roubo bookstand (page 50); **Jim Robinson** Office shelf (page 55), Peg rail (page 93); **Andy Standing** Desk set (page 64), Key cupboard (page 104), Window box (page 115), Shove-halfpenny board (page 150), Toy rocking chair (page 158).

GMC Publications would also like to thank the editors of the following magazines, in which earlier versions of all the projects were first published: *Woodworking Crafts*, *Furniture & Cabinetmaking* and *Woodworking Plans & Projects*.

SUPPLIERS

Axminster Tools & Machinery
Veritas centre marker
www.axminster.co.uk

The Beaderie
⅛in (3mm) natural leather
www.thebeaderie.co.uk

Festool United Kingdom
Domino loose-tenon joiner
www.festool.co.uk

General Finishes
Water- and oil-based finishes
generalfinishes.com

Hobbies Ltd
Moulded disc wheels
www.alwayshobbies.com

iGaging
Digital callipers
www.igaging.com

Lee Valley Tools
Tools and hardware; Veritas centre marker
www.leevalley.com

Liberon Ltd
Woodfinishing products incl. French polish
www.liberon.co.uk

Mafell
Mini circular saw
www.mafell.de

Mirka
Abranet abrasive products
www.mirka.com

Osmo UK
Wood finishes incl. Osmo hardwax oil, Polyx-Oil
www.osmouk.com

Power Adhesives Ltd
'Mouseplane' flush plane tool
www.mouseplane.co.uk

Rockler Woodworking and Hardware
'Bench Cookies' workpiece grippers
www.rockler.com

Screwfix Direct
Hardware incl. roofing bolts, cross-dowels, PTFE tape
www.screwfix.co.uk

Trend Machinery and Cutting Tools Ltd
'Loc Blocks' workpiece supports
www.trend-uk.com

INDEX

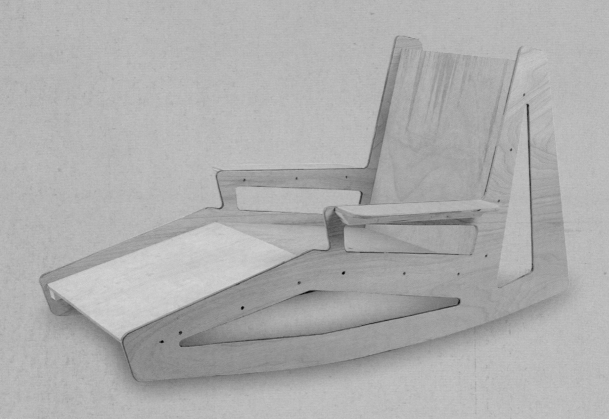

To order a book, or to request a catalogue, contact:
GMC Publications Ltd
Castle Place, 166 High Street, Lewes, East Sussex
BN7 1XU, United Kingdom
Tel: +44 (0)1273 488005
www.gmcbooks.com